COLORADO
OUTDOOR LOVER'S
GUIDE

EDITED BY NIKI HAYDEN
FRONT RANGE LIVING

FULCRUM PUBLISHING
GOLDEN, COLORADO

ISBN 1-55591-495-0
ISSN 1544-3787

Editorial: Marlene Blessing, Daniel Forrest-Bank, Alison Auch
Cover and interior design: Anne Clark
Lower left cover image: Copyright © Dugald Bremner/Getty Images.

Printed in Singapore
0 9 8 7 6 5 4 3 2 1

Fulcrum Publishing
16100 Table Mountain Parkway, Suite 300
Golden, Colorado 80403
(800) 992-2908 • (303) 277-1623
www.fulcrum-books.com

■ SPRING

These celebrated cranes migrate every spring and fall through the small farming community of Monte Vista in southern Colorado.

The sandstone bluffs are the Pawnee Buttes. The unbroken vista is Pawnee National Grassland. Together, they're one of Colorado's best-kept secrets.

The only way to really get a sense of the Medano's untamed beauty is to drive out on a primitive road that in spring is a bone-jarring adventure.

On nearly any spring day, you can find an exquisite blossom, from the dainty lavender pasqueflower with paper-thin petals to the gaudy late summer brown-eyed Susan.

■ SUMMER

You don't have to be an Olympic-caliber athlete to hike one of these majestic peaks. So if you've never been to the summit of a fourteener, now's the perfect time to try.

Colorado is home to more species of butterfly than anywhere else in North America, and El Paso County is home to most.

Alpine streams and meadows, mature aspen forests, and expansive tundra vistas skirt high mountain passes between fourteen-thousand-foot cliffs. The dramatic rise in elevation provides a continuous show of flowers.

Like the mining site that bears its name, the word "matchless" also suits a story that could have been conjured up for a film, had it not actually unfolded in Leadville.

CONTENTS

What makes it so wonderful is that it's a challenge, and there is a certain amount of delicate expertise to be learned. But you can catch a fish on the first day.

Vail is snowy glitz in winter, but when summer arrives, the crowds thin and bicycles replace skis. And while Vail is famous for adventurous mountain biking, there also are fourteen miles of paved trails.

Colorado is a land of rock—breathtaking walls of rocks, streambeds of pebbles, sculptured mountain tips, lichen-covered boulders, and gravelly scree that makes up a thin layer of soil.

Hundreds of birds live in the giant cottonwoods and willows that surround Barr Lake, and the closer you get, the louder the broadcasting of trills, caws, chirrups, whistles, and melodies.

▪ AUTUMN

Not quite warm enough for water sports. Not nearly cool enough to hit the ski slopes. But September and October are the perfect months to make a weekend trip to one of Colorado's many inviting hot springs.

Wild mushrooms must be collected from the forest and cannot be cultivated on a mushroom farm. The exquisite, tender chanterelles or the robust, meaty boletus rarely are found fresh in stores. They're discovered in the mountains of Colorado.

Those stalwart grasses with unremarkable flowers held aloft need only catch a slight breeze to continue their species.

As temperatures begin to drop, balloonists gather along the Front Range for airborne festivals. Traveling by balloon gives a bird's-eye view of spectacular scenery.

■ WINTER

Bats may be hibernating, but winter brings other changes to those out and about. In winter you'll see plant and animal relationships that would rarely be noticed any other time of the year.

Full moons make for perfect nighttime hiking. They offer enough illumination for you to see the trail and the beauty that surrounds you at a quiet time.

The lure can be enticing for someone who has never donned a pair of snowshoes— a snowshoe hike with a ranger for two hours of trails. During the past four years, park rangers have collected would-be snowshoe enthusiasts for hikes during the winter months.

It's a place where bald eagles soar, mule and white-tailed deer cavort, and coyotes compete with foxes for food. You could spend an entire day here and rarely see another human being. And this serene, natural retreat is right in the middle of— Commerce City?

Getting raptors back on their wings is the goal of the Rocky Mountain Raptor Program in Fort Collins, where injured birds are rehabilitated.

When I first met with the original writers at Front Range Living nearly three years ago, most of us had arrived from the world of Colorado newspapers. All of us had experience covering the daily stories of everyday life and we wanted to continue to do so—but in a different arena with a new slant. Together we hammered out the areas that we believed were of compelling interest to readers. One was the cultural world of history, design, and architecture. The other was the natural world, whether cultivated in gardens or visited on a mountainside.

We pooled our ideas and came up with a philosophy for covering the immense and spectacular terrain of Colorado. And while there are magazines devoted to environmental concerns and books devoted to extreme sports, we imagined chapters more personal, almost like a diary.

"Animals," said Dianne Zuckerman, who has always championed the feathered and furred. For this former theater critic for newspapers and magazines, the natural world is a tooth-and-claw stage, full of crises and struggles, winners and losers.

"Leisure and fun, too," said Beth Krodel, who loves to soak in a hot springs after a day of hiking. Following a stint as a foreign correspondent in the Middle East, Beth is content to find adventure closer to home.

"Learning about the rocks, plants, and land formations," was my response. No one can overlook our spectacular rocks, but I wanted to write about the smaller worlds, too—the delicate pasque flower with petals as thin as tissue, the migration of butterflies in mid-July, and the call of birds that flock around Barr Lake.

We would take our readers on journeys into our wide-open spaces and ask questions that any ordinary person might ask. And then we would report back. Not one of us is a scientist or an Olympic athlete. We would search for outdoor experiences that anyone would enjoy. And in most cases, these would be trips on which you could take a child, mother, neighbor, or friend.

When Carol Ward and I sat down to discuss how best to cover antiques in Colorado, we came with similar perspectives. We wanted to introduce our readers to the joys—and caveats—of collecting. Whether you crave the rustic lodge look or the frills of Victoriana, we would search for solid information. "Old World elegance," Carol, who loves the country styles of Europe, said, "History as it is handed down in objects and places or a prized possession that tells a story." Together we have searched for stories that cover Colorado uniquely: our love for all things Western, casual interiors that mix the old with the new, appreciation of workmanship and craft, glassware, jewelry styles, or silver serving utensils that never will be made again.

In doing so, we talked to dealers who have become experts in their fields and to collectors who have amassed a valuable group, or, more often, simply indulged in an affordable passion. Antiques are linked to our cultural history and reveal the abrupt changes in our homes, children's playthings, dining habits, entertainment, and fashion.

If antique stories divulge the small details of the past, homes and gardens tell volumes. Houses from previous generations reveal not only the strata of the wealthy and working classes, but also the dominant art of the day: arts and crafts, English Tudor, Spanish adobe, Victorian neo-Gothic. Gardens, too, are linked to the buildings they surround, like petticoats enhancing the prima ballerina. Colorado contains the comfortably worn and the cutting-edge. Heidi Anderson and I searched for old and new, grand and modest, historical and modern. Where she found recycled, renewable, revamped architecture, I found familiarity in bungalows, Victorians, and modernist design.

Gardening brings a history through the decades as well. Before drought gripped Colorado, scientists voiced concern that we were stretching our water supplies. Living in a semiarid climate, coupled with the influx of new residents, makes water conservation a hot topic for gardeners. The answer to wise planting may be in native plants that predate any people at all. Or, perhaps the old-fashioned plants that have survived adverse conditions over many decades will shape our landscape. Then, there are the newer imported plants that are drought-resistant in other climes and have successfully adapted to our own. We interviewed successful amateurs and seasoned professionals—each devoted to an informal laboratory—the garden.

Our readership grew slowly but surely. The Internet has become an effective way to provide low cost information to millions of readers—to have a personal relationship with those readers and act quickly, correct errors, and build archives of value. For a magazine, the Internet becomes an incubator. What do your readers choose? How can writers tailor their stories to readers' needs? Whether cooking fresh produce from the farmers markets or learning about growing culinary herbs, we were able to discover which stories were most popular. We followed those interests and continue to do so.

A few readers asked if we would consider collecting stories in book form. Computers, they suggested, were fine for working and researching, but not comfortable to curl up with on a cold winter night. Readers, they told us, like books, too. Now we have partnered with Fulcrum Publishing in Golden, who has guided us in the first of an extended series. We'll begin with guides to the Colorado outdoors, antiques, and homes and gardens, with more to come in the future. The old and new have conjoined. And whether you love the Internet, or prefer books, Front Range Living will give you the best of both worlds.

Paper or cyberspace—it still comes down to words and whether they engage, enlighten, or entertain us. New communications technologies alter those they push aside, but the old are remarkably resilient. The Internet won't do away with books. In fact, the two have become the newest of best friends. Front Range Living will provide an ongoing source of Colorado experiences for our readers. But when the day ends, and you want to slip under bedcovers with a cup of tea and a good book, we'll be available as a bedside companion, too.

—Niki Hayden, Editor
Front Range Living

Colorado is filled with natural wonders—so many that most of us could spend a lifetime tracking them down. But we would never see everything. That's true for a book, too. This book doesn't promise to detail everything in Colorado. Instead, it presents a select group of places and activities that are sure to soothe your soul. Most are nearby for those who live along the Front Range. You won't need to be an extreme fitness buff to indulge in any of these trips, and most are as much for children as adults. Nearly all are free or inexpensive.

A few of the activities are educational—so much so that you can read a chapter to your children and they will pick up useful, even awesome, material for a science lesson. Some are just fun, such as a soak in a hot springs or a balloon trip across the Rockies. All will make you appreciate the diverse landscape and wildlife in our region. There are resources at the end of each chapter that are worth exploring before you set out for your trip.

And here is a plea: with all the hiking, biking, and camping that goes on in Colorado, consider volunteering your time to care for our wilderness. Volunteers for Outdoor Colorado (www.voc.org) will find the right place, time, and job for you. If you're a mountain climber, consider the following organizations: the Colorado Mountain Club (www.cmc.org) and the Colorado Fourteeners Initiative (www.coloradofourteeners.org). These organizations have volunteer programs that maintain trails, which ultimately help to prevent erosion year-round.

If you yearn for a hike in the mountains, a chance to see a crane migration, or a journey through prehistoric time as captured by a canyon, you'll find a place that is spectacular. But to make that experience safe, keep in mind a few caveats about Colorado.

We are at high altitude, and that means that out-of-state friends need to take precautions. Altitude sickness is prevalent, even among Front Range residents. Children and the elderly are the most affected, but anyone who takes on a strenuous venture at a higher altitude can be plagued by the fatigue and headaches that are obvious signs of the illness. It's important to drink plenty of water when at high altitude and take it easy for the first day. If you will be out in the backcountry, be sure to check for avalanche conditions at the Colorado Avalanche Information Center's website, www.geosurvey.state.co.us/avalanche.

And always bring sunblock. High altitude means we are closer to the sun. In little time those rays can burn unprotected skin, no matter what the season.

When preparing for an adventure, most of us assume that our natural common sense will protect us, but it's surprising how often we need just the right thing to make a trip a success. Every year, unwary hikers, bikers, and travelers find themselves stranded. It can happen to anyone. But you can blunt some of the concerns by being prepared. Here's a list of what to pack, and keep, in the trunk of your car.

For winter traveling, make sure you have tire chains, a small snow shovel, extra clothing, traction mats for your tires, a bag of sand or kitty litter for extra traction, a snow brush with an ice scraper, jumper cables, and a flashlight with extra batteries. Keep an extra blanket in your car, and even a sleeping bag if you have room. Most people have cell phones, which serve to alert authorities in case of an emergency. But they often don't work outside a certain range so, by themselves, may not be reliable. Keep a cell phone adapter in your car in case the batteries wear out.

Add water and nonperishable food, such as a mix of nuts and raisins. Windshield washing fluid is essential for muddy storms, and a roll of paper towels will keep your lights clean and visible. Be sure to include appropriate maps, a fire extinguisher, and first-aid kit. Whew! It's quite a list, but one designed for most minor emergencies.

Finally, check for snowpack conditions and weather forecasts. For Denver and Boulder, call 303-275-5360; Fort Collins, 970-482-0457; and Colorado Springs, 719-520-0020. Western Slope residents in Summit County can call 970-668-0600; Vail, 970-827-5687; Aspen, 970-920-1664; and Durango, 970-247-8187.

You've done your best to plan a safe and rewarding outing. So once you've packed, relax and head out. You're ready for nearly anything that Colorado weather can throw at you.

SPRING

CRANE SPOTTING:
ON THE LOOKOUT FOR SANDHILL CRANES

by DIANNE ZUCKERMAN

A late afternoon whiteout in Monte Vista is scarcely the ideal way to catch sight of the celebrated sandhill cranes that migrate every spring and fall through this small farming community in southern Colorado.

Sandhill cranes land with outstretched legs, looking like prehistoric creatures.

But shortly after embarking upon the self-guiding auto loop that meanders through a segment of Monte Vista National Wildlife Refuge, I'm surrounded by a sudden deluge of snowflakes. On one side of the road are patches of half-frozen ponds. On the other, frosted fields stretch to the horizon. As flakes whirl down like the Furies, I'm momentarily suspended in a white-gray world, my sense of direction scrambled, wondering if I'll find my way back before nightfall.

Then the flakes stop falling as quickly as they began. I scan the sky and grassy expanses for a glimpse of the long-legged, russet-gray birds that stand almost four feet tall and have distinctive red crowns. Overhead, a trio of Canada geese are caught in an aerial obstacle course, wings straining against a strong wind. Down a nearby slope, a handful of hardy cinnamon teals skirt the ice-encrusted water. But so far, no cranes.

My first sighting of the elegant birds comes unexpectedly, as the final leg of the auto tour edges alongside wide meadows backed by bare-branched cottonwoods. Shivering from a chilly gust and wiping watery eyes, I suddenly comprehend that the smoke-colored blurs fading into darkening fields are cranes. Thousands of them. Seen through binoculars, they scratch the soil, enjoying their final bites of grain before flying to the interior sections of the 14,189-acre refuge to roost overnight in frigid, shallow ponds.

Watching the mass of sandhills that peck, strut, and preen, I spy a curved white shape at the edge of the flock. A patch of snow? With growing excitement, I focus my binoculars on a breathtaking white form, one of the two whooping cranes that travel with the Rocky Mountain population of sandhills. As night swoops into the San Luis Valley, my first day of crane-spotting shifts from frustrating to memorable, a fitting introduction to the wonder of avian migration.

Monte Vista National Wildlife Refuge was created in 1953. But the cranes—whose huge, three-toed feet first trod the world's wetlands at least forty million years ago—have probably been migrating through Colorado for centuries.

SANDHILLS RETURN TWICE EACH YEAR

"It's like an hourglass," says Ron Garcia, deputy manager at Monte Vista and Alamosa National Wildlife Refuges. "Their nesting ground covers several states. Their wintering ground is fairly large as well. But they all bottleneck through the San Luis Valley during the fall and the spring."

The Rocky Mountain population of sandhill cranes consists primarily of greater sandhills, with a scattering of lesser sandhills and Canadian sandhills. The birds usually arrive in mid-February and remain through the end of March. From April to August, the flock nests in the Greater Yellowstone

The arrival of the cranes has sparked a festival, held each year in the town of Monte Vista.

Leftover grain lures the cranes, along with the Rio Grande River marshes, which offer sanctuary from predators.

area—Idaho, Montana, and Wyoming—with the largest concentration centering on Grays Lake National Wildlife Refuge, a remote, marshy plateau near Pocatello, Idaho. The cranes trumpet back through Colorado from early September through November en route to wintering grounds at Bosque del Apache National Wildlife Refuge in New Mexico.

What turned placid Monte Vista, population about 4,300, into the cranes' major stopover point? "The attraction is the small grains, the wheat and barley," Ron says. But fields of waste grain—the leavings that remain after harvesting—aren't the only lure. "You have to have a combination of things," he explains. The ideal mix is sufficient grain and water—the Rio Grande River winds through the valley—and close proximity to roost sites, such as ponds that dot the refuge. The absence of adjacent grain fields is why the Alamosa refuge, only about twenty miles away, doesn't attract the cranes.

CRANES LOSING HOMELANDS

Sandhills traditionally protect themselves from coyotes and other predators by overnighting in low water, such as the ponds at the Monte Vista refuge. But predation isn't the major threat during migration, Ron notes. "Most of their mortality comes from collisions [with] power lines."

The greatest danger of all is disappearing wetlands due to development, which in turn

Thousands of cranes fill the sky like feathery parachutes.

affects the cranes' total population. The survey count is done in the fall, after breeding season. For the past few years, the Rocky Mountain population of cranes has ranged between 18,000 and 22,000, which seems to be the maximum number of birds that can be supported by existing habitat. "Above that, it becomes stressful," Ron says. "So the goal is actually to keep them in that range."

Natural mortality and decreased breeding linked to cycles of drought play a role in population control. So does hunting. While greater sandhills are a protected species in Colorado, "some of the states around us do hunt them. That's why they do the production surveys, to let the states know how much, or if they can hunt them at all. When the numbers are up, hunting's allowed."

Lords of the fields, the cranes stalk through the farmers' tilled rows.

Although the concept makes sense when discussed in the abstract, as I watch the regal cranes streak off at sunrise the next day, I find it difficult to envision someone shooting down such beautiful creatures. Bodies straight as arrows, their wings span five feet and flap like smoothly synchronized fans. As clusters of birds head out for breakfast, the resultant percussive rustle is accompanied by a unique bugle, a kind of combination trill and quack that makes a crane's call one of the most difficult to imitate.

Farmers Help Cranes Survive

The birds usually feed on grain early in the morning and late in the afternoon. The rest of the time is spent in so-called "loafing" areas, wet meadows where they rest up and supplement their diet by scrabbling for mice, worms, insects, and frogs.

Drive down any of the two-laners that link the area's farms, and you'll probably spot segments of the flock, stalking about as though lords of the field, which they are in a way—one-half the participants in what Ron characterizes as a "win-win situation" for the avian visitors and human residents dependent on agriculture.

"The birds come in the spring before the farmers have planted, so there's no conflict. And they come in the fall after they've harvested, so there's no conflict. A lot of these farmers are switching crops—barley, alfalfa, and potatoes. And when they're rotating to a different crop, they don't want to have a lot of waste grain sprouting the next year. So the more the cranes eat, the less [the previous grains] come up in their new crop."

The most picturesque, close-up spot to watch the birds is an observation pull-out at the southwestern corner of the refuge. The grain field there, planted by refuge personnel, is surrounded by the Sangre de Cristo Mountains, dominated by massive, snow-draped Blanca Peak.

Late afternoon brings a cacophony of cranes in flight. Wings spread, twig-thin legs outstretched, their huge feet poke out like released landing gear as they float down, a skyful of feathery parachutes. As thousands more arrive, the cranes flutter about, eating and periodically breaking into an enchanting display of "dancing."

Jumping, bowing, and the fluttering of wings may be courtship gestures.

The mesmerizing movements—jumps, bows, a showy spread of wings—are thought to be linked to courtship and pair-bonding among the cranes, which mate for life. At times, the dancing looks expert and decidedly aggressive. A couple of cranes suddenly bound into the air, seemingly intent on vanquishing one another with an intriguing combination of grit and grace. Other times, the standoff looks so awkward and inept that the participants must surely be younger, less-experienced birds having a fling with maturity.

As feeding time draws to a close, the cranes usually take off in small groups. But shortly before sunset, something—perhaps a high-flying and much-feared eagle—triggers a massive departure. Without warning, the cranes cease feeding and straighten, heads still, bodies alert. Suddenly they fly up, silhouetted against a fading sunset. As alpenglow suffuses the perimeter of peaks behind the silent, abandoned fields, the cranes slowly disappear, distant specks gracing the waiting sky.

Thousands of cranes in flight claim the skies of Monte Vista.

WHOOPING CRANES

At nearly five feet tall, with ebony-accented white feathers, bold red patches adorning sleek heads, and a wingspan of seven feet, whooping cranes are stunners. They're also highly endangered.

As of July 2000, throughout the United States and Canada there were 265 whooping cranes in the wild and an additional 122 in captivity. The main wild flock winters in Port Aransas, Texas, and the biggest concern is that a single disease or natural disaster could wipe out that entire population. For this reason, attempts have been made to establish additional self-sustaining flocks, such as an effort to integrate whooping cranes into the Rocky Mountain sandhill population.

In 1975, the U.S. Fish and Wildlife Service and the Canadian Wildlife Service began a cross-fostering experiment to see if the sandhills would raise young whoopers. Eggs from captive whooping cranes and the wild population breeding at Wood Buffalo National Park in Canada were transferred to greater sandhill crane nests at Grays Lake National Wildlife Refuge in Idaho.

Initially, the effort seemed on the brink of success, as many cross-fostered whoopers survived and migrated with the sandhills. But by 1989, no pairing or reproduction had occurred between whooping cranes, presumably because of improper sexual imprinting, a problem noted in other foster-reared species. Efforts to increase the number of whooping cranes have shifted to eastern locales, such as Kissimmee Prairie Preserve State Park in Florida.

Given the similar needs and habitat of whooping cranes and sandhill cranes, why do only the sandhills seem to be thriving? Ron says much of the answer involves disappearing wetlands.

"Both species are monomorphic," he says, "meaning both sexes are the same color. And they don't conceal their nests; they nest on mounds. Sandhills nest primarily in beaver ponds and forested areas, so they can somewhat camouflage [their nests]. But a whooping crane, being bright white and nesting on a mound that literally can be seen forever...."

Seen against a Colorado sunset, sandhill cranes fly with wings arched, black forms against vivid color.

No pun intended, the whooper eggs and chicks become sitting ducks for predators, such as coyotes. "So part of what the whooping crane needs," Ron explains, "is somewhere that's free of predators. And right now, the only nesting population is in Wood Buffalo National Park in northern Alberta. That park is literally thousands of acres of wetland. In some portions, there is no access by land-based predators." But aside from a very few such sites, "these large wetlands just don't exist anymore."

If current efforts to save remaining wetlands and establish additional populations of whooping cranes don't succeed, there's a sobering possibility that one day, the majestic whooper could cease to exist.

■ BIRD AND WILDLIFE REFUGES

Alamosa/Monte Vista National Wildlife Refuge, U.S. Fish and Wildlife Service, 9383 El Rancho Lane, Alamosa, 81101; 719-589-4021; http://mountain-prairie.fws.gov/alamosanwr.

Bosque del Apache, National Wildlife Refuge, P.O. Box 1246, Socorro, New Mexico 87801; 505-835-1828; http://southwest.fws.gov/refuges/newmex/bosque.html. Wildlife refuge that is home to sandhill cranes, too. Their Festival of the Cranes is November 19 to 24.

■ HELPFUL ORGANIZATION

Audubon Colorado, 3107B Twenty-eighth Street, Boulder, 80301; 303-415-0130; www.auduboncolorado.org. Has numerous local affiliates. For excellent page of related links, go to www.auduboncolorado.org/birds.htm.

■ RECOMMENDED READING

Cranes, The Noblest Flyers by Alice Lindsay Price (La Alameda Press, 2002).

■ WEBSITES

www.birding.com. Comprehensive site for the amateur birdwatcher.

www.birdingpal.com. Connects you to local birdwatchers worldwide.

www.birder.com. Provides birding checklists for all states.

www.birdwatching.com. Comprehensive birding site spanning backyard techniques through equipment.

www.narba.org. North American Rare Bird Alert.

◼ Pawnee National Grassland: The Other Colorado

by DIANNE ZUCKERMAN

Think of Colorado, and mountains come to mind. But the eastern part of the state has a very different look—what travel brochures tout as the "other Colorado."

High plains sweep toward a serene horizon. Dusty, drought-prone panoramas were part of what pioneers called "The Great American Desert." In

A sandstone bluff is the destination of a near-solitary hike.

place of craggy peaks sporting pine-green skirts, imagine wind-scraped bluffs dominating endless open space.

The sandstone bluffs are the Pawnee Buttes. The unbroken vista is Pawnee National Grassland. Together they are one of Colorado's best-kept secrets. This is the place to go when you want a peaceful drive or near-solitary hike, far from the hordes of visitors seeking tourist-town glitz and more familiar Rocky Mountain views.

Located about one hundred miles northeast of Denver, Pawnee National Grassland is administered by the U.S. Forest Service. Pawnee Pioneer Trails, part of the state's Scenic and Historic Byways system, is 125 miles of gravel and paved roads that snake across an eroded landscape known as the Colorado Piedmont.

A PATCHWORK OF PRIVATE AND PUBLIC LANDS

The Pawnee was one of several Native American tribes that passed through the region, before Anglo settlers arrived around 1861 and usurped the land after deciding it might sustain cattle, sheep, and a few crops. Which it did—until the 1930s, when Dust Bowl clouds blew away the inhabitants' livelihood. As farms failed, the federal government began purchasing parcels of land that eventually were transformed into Pawnee National Grassland in 1960.

Pawnee National Grassland was the result of land too harsh for pioneers to farm.

The hardiest settlers managed to hang on to their homesteads and pass them down to sturdy descendants. As a result, the area today is a patchwork of public and private lands. As you drive along Pawnee Pioneer Trails, marked by blue signs displaying a columbine—the state flower—you'll glimpse grazing cows and ranches isolated as islands.

Visit in late spring, when the short-grass prairie explodes in multiple shades of green, and you might come upon brown and white Hereford calves behind roadside fences. Milky faces give them the painted look of solemn, soft-eyed clowns. The skittish youngsters are quick to scamper off at the whine of a passing car.

ON A CLEAR DAY YOU CAN SEE FOREVER

Pawnee National Grassland encompasses two sections that together cover 193,000 acres, a thirty-by-sixty-mile tract in northeast Weld County. On the western side of the grassland, just north of Briggsdale, Crow Valley Recreation Area includes a pleasant primitive campground set down amid the cottonwoods. The Pawnee Buttes to the east are closer to Raymer, one of several small towns that dot the area.

Driving across the grassland, a region given central billing in James A. Michener's novel *Centennial*, is the best way to get a sense of its overall size and topography. Afternoon summer thunderstorms can blow up quickly and fiercely, making morning—or better yet, spring or fall—the best time to arrive.

On a clear day, it seems you really can see forever, or at least to Nebraska and Kansas. Cobalt blue skies make a perfect backdrop for snowy clouds floating overhead like wide-bodied blimps, their shadows brushing the arid land. But there's enough rain here—twelve to fifteen inches annually—to provide a changing parade of wildflowers.

A Short-Grass Prairie Region

Perky black-eyed Susans, puffy thistle blossoms, and white evening primroses that line the road are just the leading edge of some four hundred plant species that thrive in the short-grass ecosystem.

A remnant of the prairie, the grasslands are home to a unique collection of mammals, birds, plants, and insects.

The grasslands are also a bonanza for birders, who can lift binoculars in search of more than 260 documented species. Even the casual observer can appreciate the avian abundance, with numerous sightings of nimble red-winged blackbirds, brown thrashers fussing noisily in the underbrush, and charcoal-hued lark buntings—Colorado's state bird—flashing their white wing patches.

Current wildlife ranges from prairie dogs to pronghorn antelope, which delight the viewer as they leap off on pogo-stick legs, the quintessential symbol of the open range. Long-ago creatures included ancient horses and a rhinoceros-like titanotheres, whose fossilized bones were excavated by a team from the Denver Museum of Nature and Science.

Representing human history, the town of Grover is located near the center of the grasslands. Incorporated in 1916 with a population of 250, the small community now harbors about one hundred people. With its mix of weathered structures, a modern brick school, and its own post office, Grover has sufficient amenities—including a small cafe and market—to give it the air of being an oasis in a landscape of solitude.

In contrast, Keota, less than fifteen miles away, is nearly a ghost town, most of its buildings reduced to forlorn abandoned farmhouses. Some ten miles to the east, the Pawnee Buttes rise 250 feet above the prairie, reaching an elevation of 5,375 feet.

Hiking Trails Abundant

A one-and-one-half-mile public hiking trail (no motorized vehicles or mountain bikes allowed) takes visitors to the base of the West Butte, which has a somewhat flattened summit. The East Butte, which curves around like a castle tower, is about a half mile farther. Because this stretch crosses private land, hikers should stay on the trail and respect the owner's rights.

Windmills that pump water into adjacent tubs for use by animals can be spotted throughout the grasslands. One of these windmills marks the overlook to the buttes. As I drive up to the trailhead on a late spring morning, the air is clear, the sun is hot, and so far, I'm the only car in sight. Smeared with sunscreen, I juggle a notebook, tape recorder, water bottle, and photography equipment as I head out. The initially narrow trail winds down toward a lush, blue-green expanse that includes blue grama grass, Colorado's state grass.

A large sign notes that eagles, falcons, and hawks nest on ledges along the cliffs a short distance from the route leading to the main buttes. Because raptors will abandon their chicks if frightened off, a separate trail branching toward the cliffs is closed annually from March 1 through June 30 to avoid disturbing birds of prey.

Hiking toward the buttes, I pass plentiful spiny yucca plants, their white blooms looking like giant bunches of grapes. I slip through an opening in a narrow fence and descend a trail that drops like sandy steps, as the supposedly "flat" landscape reveals more complex contours, dipping and rising with raw appeal.

Beneath the trail is a ravine where a wide gully twists around, past scrappy bushes and surprisingly tall evergreens. The tan and green terrain is brightened by bursts of violet-toned Rocky Mountain locoweed and

Because you may see only a few hikers, it's a time to savor the quiet beauty.

orange butterflies flitting about the vegetation. Rounding a curve in the trail, I'm startled by the sudden cries of a circling magpie, perhaps protecting a nearby nest.

On past visits, I've seen horseback riders trot down the trail to stand out on the horizon like western film heroes. Today, though, only a few hikers are in sight on the prairie.

As the temperature rises, bird whistles give way to insect hums, the buzz so loud it sounds like wires about to pop. The heat can coax out reptiles, including infrequently seen rattlesnakes or—more commonly—large beautifully patterned bull snakes, like one I previously saw slither into the brush a few yards from the West Butte.

A SETTING FOR SOLITUDE

Because of their fragile, crumbling surfaces, climbing on either butte is discouraged. Better to stroll around the base, absorbing the landmark's dramatic looks as you contemplate how the West Butte, when seen from behind, looks oddly like the back of a frizzy-haired head, or perhaps a mushroom mounted on a platform.

With the sun almost straight overhead, the flowers are wilting and so am I. Admiring the East Butte from a distance, I turn and retrace my steps. Back at the parking area, several vehicles are now baking in the sun. I'm finished for today, but I'll return again to repeat an earlier, rewarding adventure.

On my first visit a few years ago, the campground unexpectedly was filled. So I took advantage of the policy that permits camping anywhere in undeveloped areas on the grassland. As the setting sun turned the landscape red, I pulled my van on to a solitary space overlooking the buttes and settled down for the night.

A coyote's wild yip provided perfect end-of-day music. Avian twitters ushered in twilight. A single moo split the hush. Darkness swallowed the buttes and serenity permeated the air, palpable as a summer blanket.

Above me, stars shone with the confidence of celestial bodies that don't have to compete with human-made lights. I stood alongside my van, imagining it to be a prairie schooner. Cooled by a soft breeze sweet with the smell of unspoiled nature, I realized this was as close as I'll get to experiencing what it was like for pioneers who once passed the night in a wagon on a wide-open continent.

RESOURCES

■ GENERAL INFORMATION

Pawnee National Grassland Administrative Offices, 660 O Street, Greeley, 80631;

970-353-5004; www.fs.fed.us/arnf/districts/png.

■ RECOMMENDED READING

Land of Grass and Sky by Mary Taylor Young (Westcliffe Publishers, 2002).

The Meadow by James Galvin (Henry Holt, 1993).

■ WHERE THE BUFFALO ROAM: THE MEDANO–ZAPATA RANCH

by DIANNE ZUCKERMAN

Standing out like a beacon against an overcast early morning sky, the big sign graced by an illustration of a bison announces the entry to the Medano–Zapata Ranch in the San Luis Valley. The image is a perfect symbol for both the site and the efforts of The Nature Conservancy, which purchased the ranch—its largest biologically significant landscape in Colorado.

While the Medano–Zapata is private land and not open to the general public on a daily basis, classes and seminars are offered.

The picture of the great shaggy buffalo represents the preserve's working bison operation. But the image is equally apt as a reminder of how concerned, committed people can help the natural world survive, despite human beings' past environmental mistakes.

Before the great westward migration began, bison—also interchangeably referred to as buffalo in North America—numbered between 50 million and 100 million. But by 1889, about the time historian Frederick Jackson Turner was penning his landmark essay exploring the passing of the American frontier, the number of bison had been reduced to one thousand, spread among a few scattered habitats.

Today, after concerted efforts by many different groups to protect and preserve the species, North American bison number more than 200,000, most of them in private herds. The Medano–Zapata herd contains some two thousand free-roaming bison. This morning, ten are grazing alongside the bumpy dirt road that winds a few miles toward a hodgepodge of buildings, among them a farmhouse that serves as the conservancy's on-site office.

While the massive, muscular bison immediately catch my eye, the landscape itself—a mountain valley at an elevation of about 7,500 feet—appears far less impressive. Endless acres of dull, gray-green rabbitbrush and greasewood stretch toward the Sangre de Cristo Mountains that jut along the horizon. But looks can be misleading. There's much, much more here than initially meets the eye.

MEDANO–ZAPATA: A KEY TO BIOLOGICAL DIVERSITY AND ARCHAEOLOGY

"This valley is incredibly unique, biologically speaking," says Sharyl Massey, the conservancy's education and outreach coordinator for the San Luis Valley. The terrain—arid but with plentiful groundwater that rises to the surface because of an unusual geological formation—supports a wealth of plant and animal life, including two hundred types of birds, a wide range of mammals, rare botanical specimens, and endemic insects found nowhere else.

The property's distinct ecology fits perfectly into the conservancy's mission. "The goal is to protect biodiversity," says Sharyl, whose background includes degrees in wildlife management and environmental education.

The conservancy targets important sites through its work with the Colorado Natural Heritage Program, whose scientists conduct inventories of the state's plant and animal life. With a million members worldwide, the conservancy raises funds for its acquisitions through private donations, corporate support, and government grants.

In June 1999, the conservancy purchased the Medano–Zapata Ranch for $6.4 million, well below market value, because the former owner felt

The bison are at home in their natural surroundings, set against the Sangre de Cristo Mountains.

strongly about preserving the site. The parcel encompasses 100,000 acres, divided evenly between the Medano (pronounced MED-a-no) Ranch and the

Zapata Ranch to the south. Both were founded in the 1860s by the area's first permanent settler.

In addition to its ecological importance, the Medano–Zapata has cultural significance. Last summer, archaeological findings revealed a prehistoric dwelling that suggests human presence here predated the Anasazi of Mesa Verde by several thousand years.

Linked to the surrounding ranches by a dependence on deep underground aquifers, the Great Sand Dunes now is part of a larger plan.

Medano is Spanish for "sandhill" or "dune," a reference to the nearby Great Sand Dunes, now an officially designated national park. *Zapata* refers either to a family surname or a misprint of *zapato,* Spanish for "boot."

BISON: NATURAL GRAZERS FOR THE GRASSLANDS

Over the years, the properties changed hands many times. The previous owner, who had the land for about a decade before selling it to the conservancy, turned the Zapata parcel into a rustic resort complete with an inn and golf course. He also started a commercial bison operation on the Medano. To bring the site more into line with the organization's emphasis on preservation and education, the conservancy plans to continue some of these activities and redirect others.

"Having a bison operation is something new to The Nature Conservancy, because we are a nonprofit organization," Sharyl explains. "Normally, we don't operate a business." With prices for buffalo meat and breeding stock currently depressed, the bison venture, under the supervision of a ranch manager and his staff, is hardly a moneymaker. But while the eventual goal is to have the bison operation help carry the costs of preserving the property, the herd has another, greater value to the conservancy.

"Primarily the bison are seen as a native grazing species," Sharyl says. The animals crop the grass about a half inch above the ground, promoting new growth and helping vegetation flourish. Additionally, unlike cattle, bison don't overgraze. "As they eat, they walk. It's part of their nature to just keep moving."

And these buffalo have plenty of room to roam, across a landscape marked by wide-open vistas and little human presence. The only way to really get a sense of the Medano's untamed beauty is to drive out on a primitive road that in spring is a bone-jarring adventure.

"Come on, Suburban, you've never let me down before," Sharyl coaxes the hulking four-wheel-drive vehicle as it lumbers out of a muddy rut. "Our staff gets stuck all the time out here," she says. The possibility of being without wheels and encountering a one-ton bison capable of running up to thirty-eight miles per hour can lead to a potentially dangerous situation. To avoid problems, visitors can explore the site only on escorted monthly tours.

The road follows Indian Spring Creek, also known as Big Spring, an important source of water for wildlife. There aren't many animals in sight today, but Sharyl recalls an earlier excursion when the panorama included hundreds of bison and elk, a large flock of sandhill cranes that had flown over from nearby Monte Vista National Wildlife Refuge, some pronghorn antelope, and even a couple of coyotes.

The addition of the Medano–Zapata Ranch and Baca Ranch lands have helped to upgrade the Great Sand Dunes from National Monument to National Park.

Located in a serene setting, Zapata Ranch now houses educational seminars.

"It was like looking at an all-American version of the African savanna. One of the reasons I like this place so much is I come out here and I feel like man has not yet dominated this landscape. There's still such a sense of wildness here."

WATER RESERVES CRUCIAL TO WILDLIFE

By contrast, the Zapata Ranch, only a few miles from the Medano via a paved road, has the look of a tranquil mountain hideaway. Because this segment, in the shadow of Blanca Peak, has greater water reserves, the site is graced by cottonwoods, ponderosa pines, and other evergreens.

Unlike the buildings on the Medano Ranch, many of which need extensive renovation before they can accommodate students, researchers, and others the conservancy would like to host, structures at the Zapata seem in good shape.

The property includes guest rooms, a restaurant, and a workshop space that has beautiful views of the surrounding trees, trails, and meadows. Right now, the conservancy is trying to shed the site's previous label of being an inn, says general manager Francis Fitzgerald.

"Workshops and field trips, to be offered along with food and lodging, will cover natural history, archaeology, and other topics that complement the conservancy's focus on conservation.

After trying, without success, to find an independent operator to take over the golf course, the conservancy closed the facility. One possible future option for that area, Sharyl says, is to turn it into a hay meadow filled with native grasses. This could lead to a seed bank for other restoration projects or provide hay to reduce the cost of feeding 250 head of cattle on the ranch. As with the bison, the hope is that the cattle operation will help defray expenses.

While future planning continues, current efforts are focused on involving area residents as much as possible, encouraging them to participate in what the conservancy calls community-based conservation. The organization realized its stereotypical image of purchasing land and putting up a fence to preserve it wasn't the best way to foster long-term protection and conservation.

"You need to involve the communities that are within that property," Sharyl notes. To help better relate to local needs and issues, the conservancy hires staff to live in those communities. "It also enables us to serve as a model," to try new techniques and share results with locals who could benefit from the feedback.

"My job is basically bringing people here, letting the public know how spectacular this place is, and what The Nature Conservancy is doing. We want people to feel this is part of their community, that they're totally welcome to come here."

SAND, WATER, AND LANDSCAPE-SCALE CONSERVATION

The Medano–Zapata Ranch, the largest acquisition The Nature Conservancy has made in Colorado, fits into the organization's current focus on what is called landscape-scale conservation. "Historically, the conservancy has preserved pockets of land in a wide variety of places," Sharyl says. "But many species need a greater landscape. You can't recognize political boundaries, especially with migratory species. You have to work to save the entire habitat."

While this philosophy particularly affects the conservancy's international efforts, it also helps explain why the group was so committed to acquiring the nearby Baca Ranch, located north of Medano–Zapata and a crucial parcel now that Great Sand Dunes National Monument has become Great Sand Dunes National Park.

A slight climb in elevation alters plant life. Suddenly, evergreens and wildflowers come into view at the base of Blanca Peak.

Although federal legislation recently approved the transfer of status for the Great Sand Dunes, in 2000, the actual development of the park took on an urgency. "All that passed was that the boundaries [of the monument] were extended," Sharyl points out. Park status depended on several factors. "For a national monument to become a park, it needs to increase in size—and what is within that extra area has to be of great natural significance."

The conservancy agreed to allow the Medano–Zapata Ranch to be considered a private inholding within the park boundary. The addition of the nearby Baca Ranch, with its montane habitat and other notable features, also contributed significantly to meeting criteria for creating the national park.

Four hundred square miles will make up a national park that protects the Dunes, as well as the aquifer under Baca Ranch.

The catch was that the Baca Ranch, regarded as covering the richest part of the underground aquifer, has long been a source of frustration for area environmentalists. Over the years, successive owners of the property have flirted with development projects, which would include exporting massive quantities of water. This could have destroyed the natural terrain and created hardships for area residents.

The Baca sold for about $31.3 million. The federal government appropriated $10.2 million toward acquisition of the piece, with Colorado state funds, private foundations, and The Nature Conservancy raising additional funds.

The resulting national park covers four hundred square miles, protecting the dunes and the entire ecosystem around it. "That's a massive amount of area," Massey says. "And it's a better way to ensure conservation success if we can have that scale of protection."

■ **DIRECTIONS AND GENERAL INFORMATION**

For more information about escorted tours of the Medano–Zapata Ranch, which are free but require reservations, call 719-378-2356. Workshops and seminars include lodging and meals from April to October at $450–$550. Call 303-444-2985, ext. 1605, or e-mail at cofieldtrips@tnc.org.

Medano–Zapata Ranch is located in the San Luis Valley. From the Front Range, take Highway 160 west of Walsenburg to Highway 150. Turn north and continue until you reach mile marker 12 for the Zapata Ranch. The Medano Ranch is on County Lane 6 North, ten miles east of Highway 17 and four miles west of Highway 150, right next to Great Sand Dunes National Park.

■ **HELPFUL ORGANIZATIONS**

Alamosa/Monte Vista National Wildlife Refuge, U.S. Fish and Wildlife Service, 9383 El Rancho Lane, Alamosa, 81101; 719-589-4021; http://mountain-prairie.fws.gov/alamosanwr.

The Colorado Nature Conservancy, 2424 Spruce Street, Boulder, 80302; 303-444-2950; http://nature.org/states/colorado.

■ **RECOMMENDED READING**

Bison: Monarch of the Plains, text by Linda Hasselstrom, photography by David Fitzgerald (Graphic Arts Center Publishing Co., 1998).

■ FLOWERS IN THE FOOTHILLS: A FEAST FOR THE SENSES

by NIKI HAYDEN

Although Crested Butte attracts wildflower lovers in July, a quieter profusion of flowers just as remarkable blankets the Front Range—home to a wider diversity of flowers than anywhere else in Colorado. The blooms begin earlier and last longer. Often, perhaps as an antidote to fire and drought, the early bloomers offer a lavish display.

Altitude, from the dry plains to alpine tundra, provides a collection of microclimates. A warming Chinook wind creates pockets of small meadows. A single mountain may generate clouds. Springs bubble up among ancient relics of woodland plants a stone's throw from drought-loving desert blooms. "We are only twenty miles from the Continental Divide," plant ecologist Ann Armstrong says. "We also are on the edge of the Great Plains and the southern Rocky Mountains. The edge of our system is spanning two geographical provinces. These are huge landmasses. So two different kinds of habitats come together. We have a mountain backdrop with a range from fifty-two hundred to eighty-six hundred feet in elevation within a mile and a half."

A delicate pasqueflower, associated with Easter, signals spring in the Colorado foothills.

DIVERSITY WITHIN SMALL MICROCLIMATES

A foothills hike is a stroll through a geography of microclimates. On nearly any spring or summer day you can find an exquisite blossom, from the dainty lavender pasqueflower *(Pulsatilla ludoviciana)* with membrane-thin petals to the gaudy late summer brown-eyed Susan.

Ann's job is to assess the health of plants in Boulder's mountain parks. Global warming, fires, and persistent drought make her voice drop off with a sigh. But in dry years, she has witnessed a wildflower show as prolific as any. "It started off very dry," she says, "drier than I ever remember, until we had three storms. Right now the vegetation is lush, but it depends on what will happen in the summer. If it stops raining, it will dry up again." And, despite the spring storms, it's the lack of snowpack that has put us in a severe drought.

Penstemon trumpets attract a host of pollinators.

But on a June day, blue mist penstemons *(Penstemon virens)* carpet the mountain floor. Their delicate blue mauve trumpets tremble on a thin stem that rises from a bed of glossy green, pointed leaves. Penstemons hail from a vast genus of wildflowers— most in the West, where they hug dry gravelly hillsides. The larger red trumpet penstemons attract hummingbirds, whose bills are a perfect fit inside the long trumpets. But small bees love the penstemon trumpets, too. Their wide rear ends shake the flower to a rumba beat as they buzz inside for pollen.

We spy a heartleaf arnica *(Arnica cordifolia),* but only one. Ann says that the arnicas shut down during drought. It's a sign of conservation. When the plant was ready to flower, there was little moisture. It will conserve energy, saving its precious root system for next year.

Spring Rains Bring Relief

Others received a solid drenching at the right time for their flowering. The chokecherry shrub *(Padus virginiana)* is in full bloom. Like other wild berries,

A tough beauty, the wild rose is recognizable with five petals and long stamens.

it will provide food for birds and bears by the end of summer. A clump of blue skullcap *(Scutellaria brittonii)* hides in the dense shade of a ponderosa pine. And in an open valley, the bright yellow and orange western wallflower *(Erysimum asperum)* claims dappled shade.

Around a corner, the bright yellow of the leafy cinquefoil *(Drymocallis fissa)* catches our attention. "Five petals and long stamens," Ann says, indicate that it's from the rose family. Roses, even the garden variety, are only a few specimens of a vast family. Although some members of the rose family don't look like roses, the wild rose, or Wood's rose, with its pale pink petals and elegant golden stamens, is immediately recognizable. But the boulder raspberry *(Oreobatus deliciosus)* is from the rose family, too, and not related to the raspberries we cultivate for fruit.

Our trail is crushed gravel, wide enough for a sturdy fire-fighting vehicle. The pulverized stone creates a nursery for the germination of plants that need water to drain quickly from their roots. Mountain pussytoes *(Antennaria parvifolia)* rises from the rocks. Silvery gray matted leaves hug the ground, the color a giveaway that these plants like to stay dry. High atop a long stem arch furry blossoms, clustered much like the paws of a kitten. Small

The fluffy blossoms of pussytoes are so named because of their similarity to the pads of a kitten's paw.

birds will harvest their stalks and blooms to line a fuzzy, soft nest.

The trail curves slightly, as if pulling back a curtain. We've entered a microclimate where the rock wall is wetter and cooler. The hillside is covered with narrowleaf collomia *(Collomia linearis),* a mountain phlox in pink and

Blue-mist penstemons carpet a forest floor beneath ponderosa pines.

deep blue, gripping a rock surface and delivering vibrant color. Alongside is alum root *(Heuchera parvifolia),* better recognized as a relative of coralbells, the landscape beauty so coveted in English gardens. Few gardeners imagine that the coralbells they prize in a traditional cottage garden originated not from Europe, but from the Rocky Mountains. Our alum root is not so showy as its domesticated cousin, but it's just as graceful, rising from patterned leaves on tall, slender tendrils.

Ann pauses by the rock-garden wall—artfully arranged by nature. It's a dramatic setting of wildflowers that all mountain botanists glow over. Wearing a crushed cloth hat and close-up lens on a string necklace, she scrutinizes a tiny blossom. Ann has lived most of her life in Colorado, observing changes in the fortunes of plants—both for good and bad. Suddenly the bad has surfaced. Diffuse knapweed *(Acosta diffusa),* a modest-looking thug, grows at our feet by the side of the trail.

Invasive Weeds Become Thugs

"Vegetation is adaptive to disturbances," Ann says with a scowl, like fire and roads bulldozed on to forestland, "but the nonnative weeds take advantage of

Larkspur adds to the variety of blues on a spring day.

disturbed soil. They are early colonizers, typically. There is a small percentage of native plants that fit that category, but the exotics have displaced the natives in being very aggressive." Once thugs like the knapweed take over, they provide fewer plants for wildlife. The key to healthy mountains is an ongoing regeneration of diversity. With about three thousand plant species, the mountains serve as a giant laboratory. Each time a small microclimate is wiped out by weed thugs, a tiny universe is lost. Weed thugs are such aggressive plants that they quickly invade territory and prevent natives from self-seeding, or spreading through root runners. Some botanists believe that a few weed thugs, such as knapweed, actually produce a poison in their roots that kills native plants.

Ironically, some thugs once served useful purposes but eventually became uncontrollable. "Smooth brome was used for erosion control and worked too well. Now it grows along the mountain roads where wildflowers once bloomed," she says.

Deep blue larkspur *(Delphinium nuttallianum)* lines up at the foot of the mountain trail, and mouse-ears *(Cerastium strictum)* waves nearby. They grab all the attention from a more modest alyssum *(Alyssum parviflorum)*. We've reached a vista of mountains and canyons. Each side of a mountain represents a distinct climate.

"The canyons on the north side are very deep," Ann says about our mountains. "The east and west canyons are more sheltered

The West is filled with daisies such as the humble fleabane daisy.

from the wind. All these things work together. For example, we have ancient plant communities. These are eastern woodland plants that have been able to survive since the end of the last ice age. It's simply because of these topographical features. They are truly a treasure."

Ann describes a progression of wildflowers. The early bloomers appear in April. By May, a late spring season takes over. Finally, there's the long summer season that

The sulphur-flower is named for its neon yellow blossom.

ends with a flourish—summer grasses. The common lupine *(Lupinus argenteus)* has finished flowering, and there's only one tiny clump of lanceleaf chiming bells *(Mertensia lanceolata)* in bloom. Instead, we catch the brilliantly chartreuse sulphur-flower *(Eriogonum umbellatum)* and fleabane daisy *(Erigeron colo-mexicanus)*.

You'll see our Rocky Mountain holly substitute, the Oregon grape *(Mahonia repens)*, which is now a stalwart ground cover in the landscaped xeric gardens of the Front Range. Saint-John's-wort *(Hypericum perforatum)* is in bud, not quite ready for bloom.

As dusk settles, Ann looks for a sign of sedum, yellow stonecrop *(Amerosedum lanceolatum)*. It's usually in the pebbly scree that makes up Rocky Mountain soil. Found in patches, a waxy, succulent, bulbous leaf and stem hold up tiny yellow flowers. Like so many flowers in the foothills, it's not showy unless you look closely. It keeps its charms quiet to all. Only those who take the time to walk slowly will notice. But in the space of one hour, you may see more flowers in bloom than in many other places on Earth.

RESOURCES

■ HELPFUL ORGANIZATIONS

Bureau of Land Management, Colorado State Office, 2850 Youngfield Street, Lakewood, 80215; 303-239-3600; www.co.blm.gov/botany/botanyhome.htm. The Bureau's Wildflower Hotline is at 800-354-4595.

Colorado Native Plant Society, P.O. Box 200, Fort Collins, 80522; http://carbon.cudenver.edu/~shill/conps.html.

■ PLACES FOR WILDFLOWER HIKES

Arapaho Pass, Boulder County Mountain Parks, Crested Butte, Fourth of July, Indian Peaks, Pawnee Pass, Rocky Mountain National Park, Roxborough State Park.

■ RECOMMENDED READING

Colorado Flora: Eastern Slope, Third Edition, by William A. Weber (University Press of Colorado, 1996).

Guide to Colorado Wildflowers, Volume 1: Plains and Foothills by A. K. Guennel (Westcliffe Publishers, 1995).

Guide to Colorado Wildflowers, Volume 2: Mountains by A. K. Guennel (Westcliffe Publishers, 1995).

Plants of Rocky Mountain National Park by Linda H. Beidleman, Richard G. Beidleman, and Beatrice E. Willard (Rocky Mountain Nature Association and Falcon Publishing, 2000).

Plants of the Rocky Mountains by Linda Kershaw, Jim Pojar, and Paul Alaback (Lone Pine Publishing, 1998).

Alpine Flower Finder by Janet L. Wingate & Loraine Yeatts (Johnson Books, 2003).

Rocky Mountain Wildflowers: Photos, Descriptions, and Early Explorer Insights by Jerry Pavia (Fulcrum Publishing, 2003).

SUMMER

■ Colorado's Highest Country: Tackling a Fourteener

by BETH KRODEL

If you live on Colorado's Front Range, chances are you've heard of fourteeners—mountains that stand at least fourteen thousand feet tall. Fourteeners are always in the media. Environmentalists struggling to preserve them. Hikers falling to their deaths or getting struck by lightning. And extreme athletes climbing them to vie for speed records.

August is the best time to tackle a fourteener.

But you don't have to be an Olympic-caliber athlete to hike one of these majestic peaks. So if you've never been to the summit of a fourteener, now's the perfect time to try. Why? Because you'll see breathtaking views not found anywhere else. Because you'll experience nature up close—from hawks and bighorn sheep to chipmunks and wildflowers. Because it will be an accomplishment—much like running a marathon or doing a one-hundred-mile bike ride. And because you can.

August is generally the best time of year to hike the state's highest peaks. There's less snow, if any at all. Avalanche danger is usually low or nonexistent. There's a threat of thunderstorms, but they often can be avoided by heading down the mountain around noon.

Fourteeners—Always a Popular Pastime

Jennifer Tucker, education and outreach coordinator for the Colorado Fourteeners Initiative, a nonprofit formed in 1994 to protect and preserve the fourteeners, suggests hiking on a weekday. "It gives you a chance to enjoy the solitude," she says. "On the weekends, there are just so many people."

In 1997, it was estimated that 200,000 people hiked fourteeners in Colorado that year; that was a 300 percent increase over the number hiking them just a decade earlier. And Tucker, whose organization is attempting to make a new count, expects the number to be much larger now. "Outdoor recreation and climbing peaks are becoming trendier—it's the focus of car commercials and soda commercials. It's sexy," she says.

But as long as you're a responsible hiker, Tucker maintains, there's no reason you shouldn't join in the fun.

Colorado's fifty-four fourteeners are scattered throughout six mountain ranges. If you live along the Front Range, that's probably the best place to begin your adventure.

The Front Range contains six fourteeners—Longs, Evans, Bierstadt, Torreys, Grays, and Pikes—each of which can be climbed in one day from most Front Range cities. The easier of the six are Bierstadt, Torreys, and Grays, each requiring about three thousand feet of elevation gain. Mt. Bierstadt is a bit shorter in hiking distance—six miles round-trip compared with eight miles round-trip for Torreys and Grays—but Bierstadt is also steeper. Torreys and Grays, which are right beside each other, can be hiked on the same day, making for a nine-mile round-trip.

HEADING OUT FOR A FIRST TIME

I hiked Mount Bierstadt (elevation 14,060 feet) for the first time on June 10—relatively early in the season, but because it was such a mild winter and such a warm spring, the snow was gone, except at the very top. And even there, we were able to avoid it.

Dressing in layers helps one cope with fluctuations in temperature.

My friend Bryan Smith and I got a late start, leaving Boulder about 8:30 A.M. We reached the trailhead off of Guanella Pass (south of Interstate 70 at the Georgetown exit) at about 10 A.M. to begin our hike. Although most hikers at the trailhead were wearing shorts, I put on fleece pants because the wind was quite cool. Bryan wore leggings under his shorts. We both wore T-shirts underneath long-sleeve shirts and our Gore-Tex jackets. Layering is the key to maintaining a comfortable body temperature during a high-altitude hike.

Bryan had a backpack filled with two quarts of water. I carried a daypack with sunscreen, a bandanna, and another liter of water; a hat, gloves, and an ear warmer to wear at the top; and our lunch—turkey and Swiss cheese sandwiches, carrot sticks, Pringles, and trail mix of dried cranberries, nuts, and chocolate chips. As we began the hike, we could see the summit off to the east, rising from a huge field of willows. It didn't look very far away. But then we began walking.

A raised wooden walkway makes the task of crossing a dense growth of willows easier on the Mount Bierstadt hike.

First we crossed the willows—quite an easy task thanks to the cut trail and raised wooden walkway. As recently as six years ago, hikers had to thrash their way through the pesky bushes. Beyond the willows, we hiked one and one-half miles up Bierstadt's western slope, which is fairly steep in spots, but doesn't require any scrambling. We took it nice and slow up the slope, stopping to take pictures, drink water, inspect wildflowers, and soak in the views. Because the entire hike is above tree line, there's nothing to obstruct the amazing vista of snow-capped peaks to the north, south, and west. We also had brief exchanges with other hikers—a middle-aged couple from Englewood, an elderly couple

A climber takes in the beautiful alpine panorama.

from Littleton, and a young trio from Boulder.

Once we reached the shoulder south of the summit, the terrain turned mostly to rock. This helped to break up the monotony of graded slope. As we jumped from rock to rock on our way to the summit, two large black hawks swept just above our heads. We were awestruck. But we were even more impressed a few minutes later when we reached the summit and were rewarded with a gorgeous panorama.

Including stops, it had taken us about three hours to reach the top. We put on our jackets, ate our lunch, snapped more pictures, enjoyed the view, and then headed down. The descent offered us the same pretty views as the ascent, although we were able to enjoy them even more because we weren't so focused on breathing. And as always, there was much more conversation on the way down.

Back at the car, we congratulated each other on the accomplishment. After all, the top is only halfway there.

Tackling Two Fourteeners

About six weeks later, on July 22, Bryan and I successfully attempted the Grays–Torreys combination. This time, we got an earlier morning start, leaving Boulder by 7:30 and reaching the trailhead—south of Interstate 70 at the Bakerville exit—by 9 A.M. (Beware of the extremely bumpy dirt road leading to the Stevens Gulch Trailhead.)

It was a beautiful day—blue skies, sunny, and warm. This time, we took it even more slowly, because we had a dog with us, and we had to make extra stops to give her lots of food and water. The trail was much more crowded than Bierstadt's, probably because late July is a more popular time for hiking fourteeners.

Take your time with a fourteener—there's no rush.

But the other hikers were very upbeat and friendly, excited about being outside.

Our walk began in fields of purple, red, and yellow wildflowers. The trail climbs gradually into upper Stevens Gulch, then switchbacks up Grays' northern slopes right to the summit. As you climb, Grays (elevation 14,270 feet) is the rounded mound to the left and Torreys (elevation 14,267 feet) is the more majestic-looking mountain to the right.

We took a break about twenty minutes below Grays' summit for a quick snack and some water, and I was feeling quite tired, wondering if I could make it to the top of Grays and then on another hour or so to the top of Torreys.

But as soon as we reached the summit of Grays—about three hours after we began hiking—the feelings of excitement and accomplishment made me forget my doubts. At the top, we socialized with other hikers—including a seventy-three-year-old woman—for about a half hour, then headed down the saddle and up to Torreys, where we met another thirty people and five dogs.

The combination of Grays and Torreys seemed easier to me than Bierstadt alone. Perhaps because Bierstadt is steeper. Perhaps because it was later in the season and I was in slightly better shape. Or perhaps because of the morale boost involved in reaching the tops of two peaks in one day.

Anyone who is reasonably fit should be able to reach the summit of Bierstadt, Torreys, or Grays. It's simply a matter of putting one foot in front of the other, drinking lots of water, and taking as many breaks as you need.

But no matter how strong a hiker you are, you have to be smart enough to know when to turn around. Perhaps you don't feel well. Maybe the weather is turning ugly. There's no need to keep going. The mountain will be there tomorrow.

RESOURCES

■ HELPFUL ORGANIZATIONS

The Colorado Fourteeners Initiative, 710 Tenth Street, Suite 220, Golden, 80401; 303-278-7525, ext. 115; www.coloradofourteeners.org. Trail descriptions, maps, hiking tips, and more. Additional information available at www.voc.org.

Colorado Mountain Club, 710 Tenth Street, Suite 200, Golden, 80401; 303-279-3080; www.cmc.org/cmc. Information on Colorado's oldest hiking club, which offers guided hikes.

Leave No Trace, Inc., 2475 Broadway, Boulder, 80304; 800-332-4100; www.lnt.org. Important tips for minimum-impact hiking.

Volunteers for Outdoor Colorado, 600 South Marion Parkway, Denver, 80209; 303-715-1010; www.voc.org.

Check with the Colorado Fourteeners Initiative for important high-altitude hiking recommendations.

■ RECOMMENDED READING

Colorado's Fourteeners: From Hikes to Climbs, Second Edition, by Gerry Roach, (Fulcrum Publishing, 1999).

Colorado's Fourteeners: From Hikes to Climbs, Companion Map Package by Gerry Roach (Fulcrum Publishing, 1999).

■ IN PURSUIT OF THE WILD BUTTERFLY: GLIMPSING AN ELUSIVE BEAUTY

by NIKI HAYDEN

Sam Johnson is dressed in full butterfly regalia: net with long pole, brimmed hat pulled closely about the head, hiking boots, water, and zipper baggie.

Sam Johnson leads enthusiasts on a butterfly hike in Aiken Canyon.

"Baggies are the only way to go," he says, crumpling one into his pocket. "You catch the butterfly, gently place him into a baggie, and pass it around. You can handle it, but it doesn't hurt the butterfly. And then, you release him."

We're in Aiken Canyon Preserve just west of Fort Carson outside of Colorado Springs. The explosion of ordnance at the fort creates sounds of war not far away. But here, on a summer day, we're watching some of nature's silent and elusive creatures: butterflies.

COLORADO: A VAST PRESERVE FOR BUTTERFLIES

Colorado is home to more species of butterflies than anywhere else in North America. El Paso County, where we are sequestered, is home to most. "At least two hundred four species of butterflies are on record in El Paso County," Sam says, "and twenty-one hundred projected [1,600 on record] species of moths. Of course both are from the same order—*Lepidoptera*."

But there are some differences. Butterflies are brightly colored and fly in the daytime. They also fly in erratic patterns, which makes them harder to catch than moths. Butterflies are brightly patterned as a warning to birds that they are bitter tasting or even poisonous. Moths are tasty. That's why they must fly at night, when birds are sleeping. Most are camouflaged to look like the markings of a tree trunk in the daytime. Their flight is cumbersome and slow, not apt to escape a bat's notice.

Armed with this information, we set out to climb the gentle foothills, where a diverse collection of plants and subtle altitude changes create a climate appealing to butterflies. But from the beginning, we discover the overall number of butterflies is down, although painted ladies and checkered whites are up. Among white moths, the white-lined sphinx are enjoying a boom year.

In full butterfly regalia, Sam swoops and catches the elusive creatures.

An icy late-spring snowstorm killed many of the buds on this preserve. Sam shows us the shriveled blossoms of a Gambel oak. There will be no acorns for the wild turkeys this year, he laments. And the tiny caterpillars of newly hatched butterflies-to-be were probably killed, too.

Back at the field station, we had gawked at mounted butterflies, one the official state butterfly of Colorado, the hairstreak. With a wingspan of four or so inches, the iridescent blue once was an ephemeral beauty, now captured and pinned for us to admire. We could only hope to catch a glimmer in the wild.

We climb in altitude slowly, the grass stamens dripping with golden pollen, waiting for the slightest breeze to blow the yellow puffs to a neighboring plant. Striding through the grasses, Sam is swooping, netting some small prairie butterflies. We pass by a *Liatris punctata*—the prairie gayfeather—with its lavender spikes visible

The prairie gayfeather *(Liatris punctata)* contains a rich nectar source for the canyon butterflies.

above the short grasses. "I wish there were more," Sam says, for the *Liatris* attracts some of the rare butterflies. And the tiny, insignificant blossoms ooze considerable nectar—the fast food of butterflies everywhere.

A Harvest of Butterflies, Wasps, and Stinging Flies

Sam's net harvests stinging flies and wasps that prey on butterflies. They buzz angrily in the baggie, although they're not savage with humans. They'll suck out the fluids of the butterfly, though, leaving the wings and only the husk of a body. Even when desperate birds eat a butterfly, they'll usually leave the wings—those beautiful but indigestible scales.

Too big for the baggie, a monarch is held safely.

Suddenly, a magnificent orange and black streak soars overhead. We're dazzled by its speed, here and there, alighting and taking off. Sam swoops the net. "I won't have to put this one in the baggie," he says, for a small baggie won't contain the monarch. We gasp as Sam details the expeditions that monarchs embark upon: the miles of flight, their return to specific places, and the gradual loss of their habitat. All the while, the monarch is still, held firmly in Sam's experienced fingers.

Monarchs lay their eggs on milkweed plants. As prairie is bulldozed for housing, their habitat dwindles. Milkweed rarely is cultivated in home gardens; it's too wild and weedy in appearance. That explains the loss of habitat. Butterflies require both a host plant like milkweed and a nectar supply like the gayfeather for survival.

Sam releases the monarch, and it quickly becomes a blip on the horizon. We will see rare and exquisite small butterflies ahead, but none as showy.

We continue to climb in altitude, passing hardy mountain mahogany shrubs and some noxious weeds—mullein. It's hard to hate mullein, tall and

The steep rise in altitude explains why Aiken Canyon is home to a wide variety of butterflies.

stately with silvery leaves and yellow flowers. Next to it, artemisia reveals its low-water requirements by the gray-green color of the leaves. Yellow asters are in bloom. There's the red-tipped Indian paintbrush and wild chicory. Pussytoes, a silvery mat of leaves that hugs the ground, serves as an edible feast for one kind of butterfly.

The red flowers of penstemon draw both hummingbirds and butterflies. But white flowers, so spectacular in moonlight, will attract moths for night pollination. We pass cacti already spent with bloom, lichen-covered rocks, and chokecherries. We pause to look at a piñon tree, its green cones covered in a piney superglue. "That's a defense," Sam says, for pests will not crawl or lay their eggs on such a sticky substance.

THE STRANGE LORE OF BUTTERFLIES

We pause for lunch, and a tiny gray hairstreak sits on a hiker's finger. It's not uncommon for butterflies to alight on us, Sam says. Perhaps they're males, who collect salts, apparently a necessary nutrient for mating. Our sweating brows could offer that. But the gray hairstreak remains for ten minutes resting comfortably, unconcerned by our peering eyes.

Butterflies may only look as if they're nature's baubles: a bit of jewelry in the wilderness. Not so,

A tiny gray hairstreak sits comfortably on a finger.

Sam says. Each species provides a specific function—no matter how tiny or insignificant it may appear.

Sam's favorite story is that of a small blue butterfly. In the caterpillar stage, it is protected by ants. Protected and, of course, exploited. In the daytime, the ants hover around the caterpillar, feasting on a sticky substance the caterpillar oozes—a kind of meringue or honey that ants adore. At night the ants are so protective

A baggie allows naturalists to observe a butterfly without damaging delicate wings.

that they hoist the tiny caterpillar over their collective ant shoulders and carry it into their den. There they sleep, keeping one eye open to guard. In the morning, the caterpillar is carried back to the sunny leaf so that it can chew, grow, and spin a chrysalis.

Only Males Matter for Science

In the meadow we see a silver spot Aphrodite with silver and black markings. And there's a crescent spot. With black, yellow, and chocolate markings, it looks like an elaborate stained glass window. A wood nymph darts in the bushes, and Sam catches a skipper. It looks rare—a dusky-winged skipper—but not worth keeping, he says. A female is worthless for taxonomy purposes. Butterflies are identified by the male genitalia—so complicated that it will determine a species when every other body part is deceiving.

"The males have hooks and spines, brushes—all because it may take hours to

Moths, as night creatures, pollinate white flowers, which show off vividly in the moonlight.

mate, and they can't simply be frightened off or they'll have no offspring. The genitalia are most complex in fleas," Sam explains, and then adds in wonder, "You have to ask yourself—what do they do with all of that?"

Butterflies disperse widely after they emerge from their cocoon. And that presents a problem. How do they find a mate if they are spread so thinly? "They all fly up, up in altitude," Sam says. "The males are up first, waiting for the female to arrive. The females fly up, meet, and mate. Then they fly down and lay their eggs at a lower altitude."

At our feet is a small hole in the ground, a tarantula home with spider silk stretched around the entrance. Sam uses a long, fine grass stem to tease out the tarantula. We stand back, in awe and a bit alarmed. But the spider never takes the bait. The disappointment shows on Sam's face. "Perhaps a tarantula hawk got him already," he says.

Sam teaches science in a Colorado Springs school. He also researches the wildlife of the Aiken Canyon Preserve. He has set out a moth trap, something he

A crescent spot, with its orange and chocolate markings, lands on a prairie gayfeather blossom for nectar.

doesn't like to do. It kills everything, he says, but there's no other way to get an accurate count of the moths. Few entomologists like Sam catch and pin butterflies anymore. They're more likely to photograph them, or use high-powered binoculars. But sometimes insects have to be put under a microscope for intensive study.

Back at the field station Sam reveals the trap's results, a bucket of moths. "You have a bucket of moths?" we ask in astonishment. "Well, not exactly a full bucket," Sam admits, but a small bucket is turned upside down on the table. Perhaps three hundred dead moths have been captured and asphyxiated for study. Most are brown and gray with fuzzy bodies. A few are white with tiny black stripes; perhaps these moths are suited for hiding on the branches of aspen trees or light-colored rocks. A few moths are pale green. But one catches his eye. "It's a *Stamnodes fervefactaria*," he exclaims. "I haven't seen one in thirty-five years!"

Sam recalls the place and year that he last saw such a moth. Outside, the day is heating up and the loud booms of artillery can be heard in the distance. We're hot and sweaty after a five-hour walk. As we head toward the parking lot, butterflies are darting from rabbitbrush to asters. Aiken Canyon Preserve is best known as a bird sanctuary, drawing hundreds of bird fans several times a year. But in the circle of butterfly watchers, Aiken Canyon hosts a stage show each July for the smaller winged that rivals anywhere else on the continent.

RESOURCES

■ DIRECTIONS

Aiken Canyon Preserve, located on Colorado Highway 115 outside of Colorado Springs. Go south on the highway to Turkey Canyon Ranch Road. On the left is the Wild Horse Saloon. Three-quarters of a mile farther south is the road on the right, Turkey Canyon Ranch Road. (Pets are not allowed.)

■ GENERAL INFORMATION

Managed by The Nature Conservancy but open to the public on weekends. Best time to watch butterflies is July through the first week in August.

■ HELPFUL ORGANIZATIONS

The Colorado Nature Conservancy, 2424 Spruce Street, Boulder, 80302; 303-444-2950;

    http://nature.org/states/colorado.

North American Butterfly Association, 4 Delaware Road, Morristown, New Jersey 07960;

    www.naba.org.

■ OTHER BUTTERFLY VIEWING

The Butterfly Pavilion and Insect Center, 6252 West One Hundred Fourth Avenue, Westminster,

    80020; 303-469-5441; www.butterflies.org.

■ RECOMMENDED READING

Chasing Monarchs: Migrating with the Butterflies of Passage by Robert Michael Pyle (Mariner

    Books, 2001).

Handbook for Butterfly Watchers by Robert Michael Pyle, illustrations by Sarah Anne Hughes

    (Houghton Mifflin, 1992).

National Audubon Society Field Guide to North American Butterflies by Robert Michael Pyle

    (Knopf, 1981).

Sex in the Garden by Angela Overy (Fulcrum Publishing, 1997).

Six-Legged Sex: The Erotic Lives of Bugs by James K. Wangberg, illustrations by Marjorie C. Leggitt

    (Fulcrum Publishing, 2001).

■ Crested Butte: A Visit to the Wildflower Capital of Colorado

by DEBBIE WHITTAKER

Long after the columbines have dropped their petals on the foothills of the Front Range, the mountains surrounding Crested Butte burst into bloom. Wildflowers awaken in the subalpine meadows of the Elk Mountains that border the town when July and early August is bloom time at ten thousand feet.

Crested Butte, a town surrounded by ostentatious blossoms, has been designated the "wildflower capital of Colorado." The showy display, along with numerous trails and varied terrain, make the locale a mecca for summer travelers, hikers, and mountain bikers, who replace winter sports enthusiasts.

The town even hosts the weeklong Crested Butte Wildflower Festival every July to honor its famous attraction; but the flowers can be seen throughout the season.

Crested Butte sits nestled in a basin in the middle of the Gunnison National Forest. Alpine streams and meadows, mature aspen forests, and expansive tundra vistas skirt high mountain passes between fourteen-thousand-foot cliffs. The dramatic rise in elevation provides a continuous show of flowers, many blooming at the same time within a particular altitude range.

A Short Season Hastens Blooms

Pasqueflowers, followed by glacier lilies, appear as early as April in the Lower Loop of Oh Be Joyful Creek, but the cycle begins

A flush of bloom covers a mountainside in Crested Butte.

later at higher altitudes. For the majority of flowers, simultaneous blooming is a requirement because the growing season is so short. Summer is a hasty visitor here, appearing around the first of July and vanishing with the first frost, as early as late August. Nature compensates for the harsh environment by selecting flowers that can bud, bloom, and seed

Colorado columbines *(Aquilegia caerulea)* blanket a hill.

quickly and by supplying an abundance of pollinators to ensure reproduction. Even the bumblebee is a common sight and the whir of hummingbirds is a constant reminder of pollination in progress.

The result is a vast display of blooms showing off their often large or brilliant splashes of color at the same time. More than a thousand species populate the area, with about a hundred boasting the more popular showy species like lupine, columbine, and delphinium. "Even seasoned scientists are amazed at the diversity of the wildflowers up here," says Ian Billick, director of the Rocky Mountain Biological Laboratory in Gothic, an independent research facility that specializes in wildflower ecology and pollination.

A wild geranium *(Geranium spp.)* is typical of the delicate flowers found at high altitude.

Gothic, a private town owned by the lab, is gateway to many of the area's most spectacular wildflower venues. A few feet beyond the town rests the parking area for Judd Falls, Copper Lake, and Rustler's Gulch. While most people park on the main road, a small parking area a half mile up the side road provides more direct access to the trailheads. Walking the rocky trail to Judd Falls provides a glimpse of dark purple monkshood, delicate light blue harebell, edible red clover, and many others that thrive in the sunny days and crisp nights.

The trail stops abruptly at the top of the falls, providing a close-up of the steep drop into the canyon. Many hikers end their trek here, returning by the same route. But a continuation of the trail winds up the side of the creek four miles to Copper Lake. Crossing streams and balancing on steep, rocky terrain make this a great adventure for equipped and experienced hikers. Beyond the lake, East Maroon Pass showcases some of the best wildflowers in the brisk solitude of 11,800 feet.

A gentian, with its deep blue blooms, forms mats of blossoms on a hillside.

Back at the upper parking lot and farther up Gothic Road toward Schofield Pass are trailheads for some less rigorous and many equally challenging routes. Other favorites include Rustler's Gulch and trails in the Maroons Wilderness Area including West Maroons Pass. On the other side of Mount Crested Butte, Slate River Road and Kebler Pass provide access to numerous other breathtaking locations. Maps and information on preparing for a day in the wilderness are available in town.

Unusual Wildflowers Also Intriguing

While Crested Butte and surrounding areas nurture more than their share of common wildflowers, other interesting species are less recognized. The monument plant, commonly called green gentian, flowers only once during its thirty-five-year life span. Buds take years to develop, and it is believed to bloom only during years with major rainfall. The striking six- to eight-foot stalks seem to bloom at the same time.

Fireweed *(Epilobium angustifolia)* takes hold after land has been disturbed—and earns its name.

One of the area's more unique plants is the rayless coneflower, an unusual variety of rudbeckia sporting a brown head that bears no petals. It grows on the west side of Kebler Pass, which boasts what some argue to be the largest living organism in the world—a mature aspen forest.

Aspen forests are created from a single tree clonally attached at the roots. This particular group spans miles of mountainside, with trees up to one and one-half to two feet in diameter, significantly wider than typical aspen.

Water is a key element of many of the microclimatic conditions that nurture the wildflowers. Mountain streams seep through rocky crags near Yule Lakes to feed what the locals refer to as moist hanging gardens of moss and monkey flower. Streambeds proffer the quirky elephant's head, with multiple blooms closely resembling its nickname. At Lily Lake, sphagnum moss and yellow water lilies grow in a fen setting. While the sphagnum moss is the same variety as that sold in garden supply houses, it takes many decades to regenerate, so "mining" is greatly discouraged.

According to local botanist Kathy Darrow, "The wildflowers are more profuse in the high alpine meadows because continuous snowmelt provides a regular supply of water." In addition, the east–west orientation of the northern section of the Elk Mountains helps retain moisture longer than the normal north–south pattern. That moisture will support more diversity. The higher you go, the greater the number of flowers because of that key element.

Aspen forests span miles, linked to water in high altitude lakes.

The short growing season in Crested Butte spurs a variety of blooms within a brief period of time.

Darrow, the author of *Wild About Wildflowers: Extreme Botanizing in Crested Butte,* the best resource for local plants, doesn't think most of the flora in Gunnison County is particularly unique. What she finds unusual is the opportunity to view plants in one of the most pristine areas in the state. Eighty percent of the land is publicly held by the state, the Bureau of Land Management, and the U.S. Forest Service, in addition to several local conservation groups. Most areas haven't been disturbed, which provides a setting aesthetically more appealing than developed areas.

Regardless of how you choose to view the flowers, Gunnison County provides access for everyone. The largest selection awaits those who are able to hike the off-road subalpine meadows, but wide expanses can be viewed from main roads on mountain passes or by four-wheel-drive access. Within the confines of the town of Crested Butte, flower-conscious residents and shopkeepers have designed beautifully planned gardens where any visitor can partake of the awe-inspiring panorama that makes Crested Butte the wildflower capital of Colorado.

Indian paintbrush (*Castilleja* spp.) is one wildflower that can be found at a variety of elevations.

RESOURCES

■ DIRECTIONS

Alpine Meadows Hiking and Backpacking, P.O. Box 1745, Crested Butte, 81224; 970-349-0800; www.alpinemeadowshiking.com.

Crested Butte Wildflower Festival, 409 Second Street, P.O. Box 216, Crested Butte, 81224; 970-349-2571; www.crestedbuttewildflowerfestival.com. More than a hundred classes, hikes, and special events. Mid-July.

Headwaters Nature Center, 620 Second Street, Crested Butte, 81224; 970-349-0974; e-mail: jclark@gunnison.com. Open June through mid-September.

Rocky Mountain Biological Laboratory (Gothic), 308 Third Street, P.O. Box 519, Crested Butte, 81224; 970-349-7231; www.rmbl.org. Open June through mid-August.

■ HIKING ON YOUR OWN

The Book Worm, 211 North Main Street, Gunnison, 81230; 970-641-3693. USGS maps.

Crested Butte Chamber of Commerce, 601 Elk Avenue, Crested Butte, 81224; 970-349-6438; www.crestedbuttechamber.com. Forest Service maps and some free handouts.

Gunnison County Chamber of Commerce, 500 East Tomichi Avenue, Gunnison, 81230; 970-641-1501; www.gunnison-co.com.

Gunnison National Forest, U.S. Forest Service and BLM Office, 216 North Colorado, Gunnison, 81230; 970-641-0471; www.fs.fed.us/r2/gmug. Topographic and Forest Service maps; pick up or phone orders.

■ RECOMMENDED READING

Beyond the Aspen Grove by Ann Haymond Zwinger (Johnson Books, 2002).

The Colorado Guide, Fifth Edition, by Bruce Caughey and Dean Winstanley (Fulcrum Publishing, 2001).

Wild About Wildflowers: Extreme Botanizing in Crested Butte by Kathy Darrow (Heel and Toe Publishing, 1998); wildkat@crestedbutte.net.

■ LEADVILLE'S MATCHLESS MINE:
A TALE WITHOUT PEER

by DIANNE ZUCKERMAN

L ike the mining site that bears its name, the word *matchless* also suits a story
that could have been conjured up for a film, had it not actually unfolded
in Leadville, sometimes called the Cloud City for its lofty elevation of more
than ten thousand feet.

But to put the tale in perspective, we need to start in a gentler clime, where
warming spring air can lull folks into forgetting that the winds of fortune can shift
as suddenly as a Rocky Mountain spring storm can swoop down with deadly force.

The old Matchless Mine, located a mile out of
Leadville, is open in the summer.

On March 1, 1883, Elizabeth
McCourt Doe, a beautiful divorcée,
and Horace Tabor, a wealthy U.S.
senator whose Colorado holdings
included bounteous silver mines, were
married in Washington, D.C., in an
ostentatious ceremony for which the
bride wore a $75,000 diamond to set
off her $7,000 gown. Fifty-two years
later—only a week past her wedding
anniversary—the impoverished and
widowed Elizabeth "Baby Doe" Tabor
was found frozen to death in her
primitive cabin alongside the
Matchless Mine, located about a mile
outside of Leadville. Between those
two headline-making events, she lived the quintessential rags-to-riches-to-rags
life that has made the Tabors' story a Colorado legend.

The Matchless Mine Revisited

The tale takes on fresh life for anyone who visits the site of the Matchless Mine, where Baby Doe's one-room cabin, with its plank floor and small potbellied stove, has been restored as accurately as possible. Old newspapers, similar to those she used for insulation, cover the walls, providing an atmospheric backdrop for historic photographs of the Tabors and other memorabilia that contrasts Baby Doe's two very different lives.

Baby Doe tried to keep out the cold by covering the cabin walls with newspaper.

Because souvenir hunters made off with many objects following Baby Doe's death, most of the period furnishings were added later. But a few authentic items remain. A delicate white silk scarf recalls the good years. So do old magazine spreads, which show a pretty woman with a rosebud mouth and a fuss of curls, her looks enhanced by expensive jewelry.

Baby Doe's later life is represented by a worn leather satchel that sits in the corner of the room and also appears in a photo taken only a few years before she died. Her most prized possession was a framed statue of the Virgin Mary, which hangs on the wall above a narrow quilt-covered bed. Baby Doe, who turned to religion and a sort of mysticism as time went by and her isolation grew, also used a calendar to keep track of the dates on which she said she communed with spirit voices. Such objects add a haunting air as you soak up the ambience of the small cabin, which was formally dedicated as a public historic site in 1953. The surrounding images add to the effect as knowledgeable guides, such as James Wilson, spin a true story that helps bring the era and the cabin's former occupant to life.

Rags to Riches to Rags

"The person we know as Baby Doe Tabor was actually born Elizabeth McCourt in 1854 in Oshkosh, Wisconsin, one of thirteen children," James begins. At age twenty-one she married a cigar maker named Harvey Doe. For a wedding present, the groom's father gave the couple a gold mine in Central City, and it's here that Baby Doe's Colorado odyssey began.

A cable-and-pulley system remains alongside Baby Doe's cabin.

They worked the mine for about two years. Showing some of the grit that would mark her later life. "Baby herself actually dressed as a man, because back then it was known to be bad luck for women to work in a mine," James says. It was also about this time that young Lizzie got her famous moniker. "At the time, Central City was kind of a grungy little mining town. Not many women would pass through. When they did, [male residents] usually had the habit of calling them Babe or Baby."

The nickname proved more permanent than the marriage, in large part because Harvey, a womanizer, preferred to work the saloons rather than his mine. So Baby divorced him and headed for Leadville, where productive ore seams—and free-spending mining men—were said to be more plentiful.

In Leadville, she struck gold—make that silver—when she met up with Horace Tabor, a one-time shopkeeper who initially grew rich by staking miners to equipment and grub in exchange for a percentage of whatever they discovered. The popular opera "The Ballad of Baby Doe" has the pair meeting as Baby sweeps graciously into the Clarendon Hotel and straight into Horace's heart. But whether or not this smitten-at-first-sight story is apocryphal, their romance blossomed in spite of several snags. The opera made its debut at the Central City Opera House in 1956 and was made famous by Beverly Sills, when she filled the role of Baby Doe in 1958 at the New York City Opera. It is considered one of the best-loved English operas of all time.

For starters, Horace, by then a silver baron perceived as having the Midas touch, had been married for twenty-five years to Augusta Tabor, whose business sense was responsible for the family's burgeoning wealth. Initially, Augusta fought Horace's demands for a divorce, and the drawn-out romantic triangle became a huge scandal. Eventually, Horace married Baby and the pair embarked upon an incredibly extravagant lifestyle.

"The Tabors were known to spend up to $10,000 a week on lavish parties, traveling, anything that caught their fancy," James says. In addition to their Leadville holdings, the couple owned a block-long mansion in Denver where one hundred peacocks strutted on the lawn. More controversial decorations included some nude statues that so offended Baby's highly proper female neighbors, "she had her dressmaker come in and make dresses for the statues."

At their height, James notes, the Tabors, who had two daughters, were one of the five richest families in the country. But it all ended in 1893, when the country moved to the gold standard. Silver—Horace's main holding, along with parcels of highly mortgaged property—came crashing down, along with the Tabors' lifestyle.

Baby Doe lived in her cabin next to the mine for the last thirty-five years of her life.

"They had to give up everything they owned, pay off these mortgages and debts," James says. Horace, in his sixties and in failing health, did physical labor for a few dollars a day until friends were able to get him a postmaster's job in Denver, a position he held until he died of appendicitis in 1899. His deathbed words to Baby Doe, so the legend goes, were, "Hold onto the Matchless."

With her two children in tow, Baby returned to Leadville and took up residence in the one-room, twelve-by-sixteen-foot structure that originally served as a toolshed. Her elder daughter, fifteen-year-old Lillie, so resented the place that she moved in with her grandparents in Wisconsin and ceased all contact with her mother and sister. Silver Dollar, a ten-year-old tomboy, lived with her mother until she grew up and left the area, embarking on a downward spiral that would lead to her premature death from drugs and alcohol.

Baby Doe, who stayed at the cabin for her remaining thirty-five years, was a proud woman who routinely refused charity of any kind. Periodically she would trudge into town for supplies, which she paid for with chunks of "valuable" ore she picked up around the property, unaware that the sympathetic shopkeepers who accepted her samples as payment probably dumped the worthless rocks as soon as she left.

The end came for Baby Doe on March 7, 1935. A snowstorm had moved into the area in late February, at which time a grocery deliveryman, the last person to see her alive, had given Baby a ride back from town and checked that she had food, water, and wood.

Other occupants in the area, who routinely kept an eye on their elderly neighbor, later became alarmed when they didn't see smoke curling up from her chimney. Two of them slogged through the six-foot snowdrifts and discovered the tiny eighty-one-year-old-woman dead and lying frozen on her cabin floor. Later reports said she had suffered a heart attack.

Baby Doe was discovered frozen and dead in her cabin at the age of eighty-one.

A COLORADO LEGEND

While Baby had heeded Horace's words and managed to "hold onto the Matchless" all her life, she never could afford to work the mine that Tabor originally purchased in 1879 for $117,000. Over a fourteen-year period, he made about $9 million. The last man to enter the mine, in 1938, reported there was still abundant silver, but not enough to justify the expense of bringing it out.

The 365-foot Matchless, located in an area called Fryer Hill, was permanently covered when the cabin was opened to the public. But you can peer down into the mine's grim, shadowed belly or look up at the wooden head frame to contemplate a rusting iron bucket used to lower miners starting a grueling twelve-hour shift, for which they were paid the grand sum of $3 a day.

The cable and pulley system that controlled the bucket was located in the nearby hoist house, which also holds a blacksmith

Although Baby Doe held onto the mine, she was never able to work it.

shop with the mine's original huge bellows. The hoist house also displays an intricately detailed scale model of the Matchless, which had seven levels, or shafts, to bring in fresh air.

Outside the small cluster of buildings, the sun brightens a deceptively mild-looking landscape, where winter temperatures have been known to drop to fifty degrees below zero. Today, aside from visitors who stop by to sample a chunk of local lore, the site belongs to wildlife such as a winsome scurry of chipmunks and chubby golden-mantled ground squirrels. Wildflowers like the purple fireweed dot the landscape, softening the harsh presence of tailing piles, century-old heaps of discarded low-grade ore.

After touring the cabin, you can further experience the surrounding terrain by driving into the winding, pine-scented hills, where the mountain's hush presses down like history and the wind speaks of lives past and futures unfathomable.

RESOURCES

■ GENERAL INFORMATION

Healy House Museum and Dexter Cabin, 912 Harrison Avenue, Leadville, 80461. Healy House hosts a play during the summer months based on the life of Baby Doe. The Museum opens Memorial Day and is closed during the winter months. The Central City Opera is located in Central City, but the administrative services and box office are at 621 17th Street, Suite 1601, Denver, 80293; 303-292-6500. Check their website at www.centralcityopera.org for information about upcoming opera productions.

Matchless Mine Cabin, 1.2 miles east of Leadville on East Seventh Street; 800-933-3901; www.leadvilleusa.com. One-hour tour is $4 for adults, $1 for ages six to twelve. Open 9 A.M. to 4:45 P.M. daily, Memorial Day through Labor Day and by appointment the rest of the year.

■ RECOMMENDED READING

The Legend of Baby Doe: The Life and Times of the Silver Queen of the West by John Burke, et al. (University of Nebraska Press, 1998).

Wild Women of the Old West, edited by Glenda Riley and Richard W. Etulain (Fulcrum Publishing, 2003.)

■ THE LURE OF FLY-FISHING: CATCHING SOME TIME AWAY

by NIKI HAYDEN

Ask a woman who knows how to cast a fishing line, and she'll tell you she learned from a man. Her husband wanted a fishing buddy. Her father wanted a son. Perhaps she slyly caught glimpses of an older brother during a family camping trip. Fishing, she decided, wasn't only a man's sport.

"Anybody can fish," Ashley Holladay says. She heads toward the Big Thompson River or Boulder County's Walker Ranch on weekends.

"What makes it so wonderful is that it's a challenge, and there is a certain amount of delicate expertise to be learned. But you can catch a fish on the first day. Women pick it up faster than men because they don't try to muscle the cast. Patience is developed."

"A good fly fisher is a good observer," says Dana Rikimaru, author of *Fly-Fishing: Everything You Need to Know to Get Started (and Keep Going)*.

"The aquatic insects are a key. You look for minnows or birds. And put up with the elements. My favorite place to fish is the South Platte River. I love moving water more than ponds; I like the sound. Mostly, I enjoy walking and wading."

Sharon Lance holds a recent catch.

Patience may be the end product of fly-fishing, but learning to handle the trout gingerly so that it's never damaged is a first lesson. Most dedicated fly fishers master the techniques of catch and release. Experts prefer barbless hooks that won't tear the trout's jaws.

They'll search under river rocks to see what the fish are feeding on and discover healthy fish to be a benefit of clean water and careful stewardship. But even a beginner can stumble over the best places to fish for the time of year, glean an awareness of the life cycle of insects, and avoid areas where fish are spawning.

Then, there's the protocol of regulations and laws that determine the number and size of fish you can catch. You may want to join a group like Trout Unlimited, which preserves creek banks, cleans up blighted streams, and educates the public.

GIVING BACK

"There's a piece of me that wants to give back to the environment," says Sharon Lance from Littleton, who fishes about sixty days a year. As vice president of the Colorado branch of Trout Unlimited, Lance is spearheading projects for wildlife preservation. "We're renovating Cheesman Canyon—gold-medal waters near Deckers. We will complete a trail that is over forty years old and revegetate the grasses that have been trampled on."

A dedicated conservationist, Sharon's biggest catch trapped her in an ethical quandary. She caught a 130-pound sailfish while on vacation in Costa Rican waters. The women's world record is 92 pounds. Her record remains unofficial because the International Game Fishing Association requires that the fish be killed. "I couldn't kill the fish," she says staunchly. "When I fish, I release all the fish."

Sharon Lance ended up releasing the one fish that might have netted her a world record.

Many longtime fly fishers practice catch and release, and it doesn't appear to blunt the thrill. "I enjoy the intense concentration, watching for rising fish," says Craige Stainton from Weld County, president of the Colorado Women Flyfishers (CWF).

Craige says that CWF has grown to one hundred fifty members in four years, and she expects it to top two hundred. They gather for trips as short as to a Longmont pond or as far as the Mother's Day Caddis Hatch, when millions of tiny flies swarm and stir up the fish in the Arkansas River. Fishing in small groups provides a safety net. If someone is stranded or falls and breaks a bone, a buddy can go for help.

"Ordinarily, I'm not a joiner," she says, "but I wanted someone to fish with. My husband is a pilot, and he doesn't have holidays or weekends. I can't plan with him to fish when the fishing is good."

Angler Shops Best Bet for Lessons

CWF is not a fly-fishing school, although Craige says it's common for an inexperienced fly fisher to join one of the more expert women and gain insight. Nowadays, angler shops host free fishing clinics, and many offer the best teachers in their area. Dana is the head instructor for classes at the Blue Quill Angler in Englewood, the first western chapter for the Vermont-based Orvis.

"I'm not very tall," she says, "so when people look at me, they can see that you don't have to be tall to cast. There's no age limit on fly-fishing. I've had students in their eighties. It's a lifetime sport. My advice is to take a class or a guide trip. You don't have to have a certain skill level. Then, just go out and do it. The best teacher is experience."

Starter kits for fishing begin at $150, but newcomers often rent from shops. And although the fervent sportswoman can spend up to $500 for a rod, it's possible to buy equipment on sale at the end of the season in late summer. To that add the cost of a license.

Freedom from Your Daily Life

Like the men who fly fish, women will speak of their experiences in hushed tones: a meditative concentration, the moment of exhilaration when the catch

is made, a calmness that a day on the river brings. Nearly all fly fishers will tell you that it's a way to get away from a job, a stressful situation, or a nagging concern.

"There's something about standing in moving water. The sound and the birds. When I'm fly-fishing, I can't think of my practice," says Sharon, a certified financial planner, "I have to focus on what I'm doing. It blocks out everything else."

"It's the freedom from your daily life, the worries and anxieties," Ashley adds. "The sound of the water and the motion of the casting, it's rhythmic and takes you out of where you might be. It's an activity that you can do with someone. You may fish apart and rejoin for lunch, swap stories, and go back to fishing for a few hours. You bond with whatever environment you are in. Then, you go home."

Catching a fish is only part of the experience: "It's the freedom from your daily life," says one fly-fisher.

(Photos courtesy of Mark Lance.)

RESOURCES

■ HELPFUL ORGANIZATIONS

Colorado Division of Wildlife, 6060 Broadway, Denver, 80216; 303-297-1192;

http://wildlife.state.co.us. Check out each year's regulations regarding fishing.

Colorado Trout Unlimited, 1320 Pearl Street, Suite 320, Boulder, 80302; 303-440-2937;

www.cotrout.org.

Colorado Women Flyfishers, P.O. Box 101137, Denver, 80250; www.colowomenflyfishers.org.

Trout Unlimited, 1500 Wilson Boulevard, No. 310, Arlington, Virginia 22209; 800-834-2419;

www.tu.org.

■ RECOMMENDED READING

Fly-Fishing: Everything You Need to Know to Get Started (and Keep Going)—a Ragged

Mountain Press Woman's Guide by Dana Rikimaru (Ragged Mountain Press, 1999).

I Don't Know Why I Swallowed the Fly: My Fly-Fishing Rookie Season by Jessica Maxwell

(Bard Books, 1998).

■ Biking the Vail Trails: One of Summer's Best-Kept Secrets

by NIKI HAYDEN

Vail is all snowy glitz in winter, but when summer arrives, the crowds thin and bicycles replace skis. "The overall character of Vail changes," says Ian Anderson, who works for Vail Visitors Center. "It's more laid-back and less scheduled. In the winter, parents are trying to get their kids into ski lessons or make dinner reservations. But in the summer, we wake up and decide what to do that day."

With fourteen miles of paved bike trails, Vail is surely one of the most bike-friendly towns in summer. In town, the auto drivers are polite, and traffic moves at neighborhood speeds, about twenty-five miles per hour. Most cyclists are polite, too, and follow good biking rules. Biking is a common, even preferred way to get around Vail, and entire families will set off on bikes. The paths intersect with streets that lead to pedestrian malls, and you'll see bike riders everywhere.

Summer is to be savored in Vail. The crowds have thinned, the air is cool, and bike paths beckon.

True, Vail is best known in the summer for perilous mountain bike trails requiring a gondola trip up to the ski slopes. But other mountain cycling experiences are available, too. Take the gondola up the mountain to the access road. This well-maintained seven-mile dirt road allows the average cyclist to meander slowly down the mountain, soaking up the views. You won't need a mountain bike for this trail, just one that's sturdy and has hand brakes.

With a day pass of $16, you'll spend an entire day jarring down the mountain. But Vail is more than mountain biking. The town offers a variety of amenities for cyclists that encourage all ages and levels of endurance. Skiers may spend a small fortune for ski passes in the winter. But for summer cyclists, the day is free.

CYCLING FOR EVERYONE

"Our principal bike path connects Vail Village to Lionshead and to Vail Pass, twenty miles to the east," Ian says for those who want to get around town. Casual cyclists cruise

Vail is best known by intrepid mountain bikers. But the bike paths attract casual bicyclists of all ages.

around town from one bike path to another. Intrepid bikers will head up the pass to Vail Summit. Once there, they can connect to bike trails that lead to Copper Mountain, Frisco, or Breckenridge.

Vail offers a park and playground for kids, an alpine garden for a rest break, and miles of bike trails through pristine valleys. Several generations could show up with bikes and find a trail for each age group. And even young cyclists will find a safe haven around the playground of the Gerald R. Ford Park. Pack a picnic lunch and the day is yours. Bring your children or head off by yourself. But first stop by one of the visitors centers on South Frontage Road in front of the mall parking structures.

Vail is compact and easy to get around. It's also well organized. The visitors centers are filled with maps, magazines, and brochures. Ask for a map of bike trails. Mountain biking brochures are small and easily overlooked, but they are available and will detail the myriad backcountry trails to choose from. Also, some paths are closed during elk-calving season, so ask about any closures.

If you have young children, the first place to visit is Gerald R. Ford Park. A bike path leads directly to a shady playground where you will also find water and bathrooms. Picnic just outside the playground on the grass, or choose a shelter with tables to spread out a lunch. It's easy to keep an eye on your kids in this park, but it's still roomy enough to give them space to run around.

Adjacent to the playground is the Betty Ford Alpine Gardens. This is the perfect respite for cyclists who need to take a break, sit awhile, and catch their breath. After all, Vail is high altitude—10,600 feet at the summit. You can't ride in the gardens, but you can lock the bike in a rack and walk through.

Besides the spectacular alpine wildflowers with native grasses in the tundra garden, there are a meditation garden and perennial garden. Admission is free, and you're welcome to return throughout the day to claim a comfortable bench.

TRY THE SUMMIT

A popular and enduring ride is the bike trail to Vail Summit. Again, a map will make it much easier to find. Following the bike trails to Summit Pass is easy once you're on it, but it begins in a residential section. You'll head toward East Vail from the park.

Vail Summit can be daunting. But you need not complete the entire pass to enjoy the most beautiful sections.

If you want to rent a bike, ask for a list of local merchants at one of the visitors centers. Most bike shops rent skis in the winter, bikes in the summer, and may offer a repair specialist on the premises. Several of the bike shops offer half- or full-day tours to Vail Pass, Shrine Pass, or Glenwood Canyon. Most offer shuttles to the top of the summit. "We typically run a shuttle about ten each morning," says Matthew

Toth, who works at Bike Tech in the Lionshead Mall.

That's because cycling from Vail to the summit is uphill and arduous. Determined cyclists wouldn't think of missing the uphill climb, but others choose the shuttle, then an easy downhill cruise from the top of the summit, coasting down the trail toward Vail.

At the summit, you'll find water and bathrooms. It's a rest area for Interstate 70 and a junction for the trail to Copper Mountain and Vail. Head west down the frontage road to join the path. You'll end

The Gerald R. Ford Park is a place for a picnic and a chance to see the spectacular plantings at the Betty Ford Alpine Gardens.

at a metal gate that blocks the way for cars. A parking lot has been carved next to the trail, and from that point on, the trail is closed to all but bike and foot traffic. It will meander closely to the highway, but doesn't intersect a road until you reach East Vail.

The most scenic portion is at the summit, where Black Lake spills into wetlands and into Gore Creek. The lake carves out a perfect alpine meadow. Wildflowers blanket the slopes—purple fireweed and yellow asters in August. Every day brings a new flush of bloom. The path ends at housing developments that look like small towns. Finally, East Vail appears, and the trail follows the Vail Golf Club, dropping you off in a residential section of Vail.

Another approach to the pass is to begin at Copper Mountain. The climb up the pass from Copper to Vail Summit is a slow, steady climb of about nine hundred feet, not the steep uphill climb of one thousand six hundred feet from Vail to the pass. The Copper trail has two entries. One is on the west side of town, past a horse stable. Parking is limited; the trail is designed for those who are staying in Copper. An alternative entry is on the east side of Copper—on the east side of Colorado Highway 91. Drive past a Conoco gas station to the end of the dirt road. An official trailhead marks the beginning of the bike trail.

MOUNTAIN BIKING

In the Lionhead Mall, it's not hard to find the line of mountain bike enthusiasts lined up for the gondola rides. They squeeze into gondolas with bikes in tow. Most riders are young men; a few wearing quilted padding, like armor, that wraps around arms and legs. All wear helmets. The only requirement is that they must have bikes with hand brakes. They'll come barreling down the mountain, zigzagging and eventually shooting through a wooden chute at the end of the ride. Then, almost immediately, they line up for the gondola again.

A gondola takes bikers up to the mountain paths. There are easy paths to meander, too.

"These bikes look more like motorcycles," Ian says, "and often cost more than the car they came in. Most are young men, although there are a few stand-out women. It has that attitude that snowboarding had years ago." The gondola runs every day in midsummer but slackens off to just weekends in early spring and late summer.

"Moab and Crested Butte are known for their mountain bike trails, but we have some that are not well known, so they are in great shape—even at the end of summer," Ian says. Son of Middle Creek Trail, Meadow Mountain just outside of Vail toward Minturn, and Two Oak at the top of Vail are the prime choices on his list. All can be found on maps.

If you rent bikes, the shops will provide helmets, but you should bring water, sunscreen, bike clothing that includes a cover for rain or cold, biking gloves, sunglasses, and snacks. It's common for late afternoon and evening thundershowers to roll into Vail, so it's wise to start in the morning and be off the mountain by late afternoon.

Vail Pass offers spectacular mountain scenery from its paved bike paths.

RESOURCES

■ GENERAL INFORMATION

Vail is most reasonably priced from late August through September. The weather usually is glorious, cool without being cold. The aspen leaves are changing color, and all of Vail seems to be a bargain for two months.

Another mountain town that offers wonderful bike trails is Steamboat Springs; www.steamboatchamber.com. Like Vail, the off-season is very reasonable.

■ HELPFUL ORGANIZATION

Vail Valley Chamber and Tourism Bureau, 100 East Meadow Drive, Suite 34, Vail, 81657; 877-750-8245; www.vailalways.com.

■ PHONE NUMBERS

Activities listing: 970-476-9090; after 5 P.M. Thursday through Saturday, 970-479-4380.

Emergency assistance if you get lost: call 1111 or 970-479-3049 from a cell phone. Wait for someone to answer, and don't hang up until the patrol tells you they have all of your information.

Vacation reservations: 800-525-2257.

■ RECOMMENDED READING

The Colorado Guide, Fifth Edition, by Bruce Caughey and Dean Winstanley (Fulcrum Publishing, 2001).

Mountain Biking Colorado by Gregg Bromka and Linda Gong (Falcon Publishing Co., 1998).

■ WEBSITES

www.vail.com. Resort site has maps, events; lists most popular activities.

www.vail.net. Dining and lodging information.

www.vailrec.com. Site designed for Vail residents, but provides information about recreation and upcoming events.

www.visitvailvalley.com. Official town visitor center's website.

Phantom Canyon: Rocks Reveal How the Earth Was Formed

by NIKI HAYDEN

"Geologists look at the landscape and see things others don't," Gregg Campbell says. "For us, one million years is a short time." Gregg stands on a bluff in northern Colorado, where U.S. Highway 287 nearly meets Wyoming. Looking across the highway we see a mountain in red layers—rock and pebbly soil, sandwiched with clay, like layers of a frosted cake. It's "part of our ancestral Rockies," he points out, a mountain of sedimentary rocks, where pressure and time has glued all together.

Ask Gregg to survey a landscape, and, in his imagination, all growing things are stripped away. That's because rocks tell geologists how the Earth was formed. Out here, in the arid Colorado rock-strewn land, the birth of the planet is revealed. "You'll have these rocks on the East Coast," Gregg says, "but you won't see them. Everything is covered in vegetation because of the climate."

Gregg is leading a tour of twelve hikers into an extraordinary canyon. But first, he dons his geologist's clothing: "A geologist is naked without

Gregg Campbell dons his geologist vest.

a vest," he says, and pulls a neon orange vest over his shirt. "This is from the days of working at road cuts, trying to stand out so you don't get hit by traffic." Geologists love to look at a new cut of land. So much is revealed in a single scoop. Pure rock, he says, unadorned by lichen—that's when a scientist gets a chance to see Earth unmasked.

ROCKS DETERMINE THE LANDSCAPE

There's no traffic where we stand. Only small herds of pronghorn antelope with necks craned, ears perked in our direction. They are curious, but not afraid. Still, they won't come any closer, and the male shakes his horns at us.

This is antelope, pocket gopher, skunk, mule deer, mountain lion, prairie rattlesnake, and golden eagle country. The antelope are drawn to the prairie grasses and open spaces. The mountain lions follow the deer. Prairie rattlesnakes keep to themselves. Eagles benefit most directly from the canyon. They soar above their ancient nests tucked into wind-eroded caves high above the river, inaccessible to anyone.

This is a land of rocks—breathtaking walls of rocks, streambeds of pebbles, sculptured mountain tips, lichen-covered boulders, gravelly scree that makes up a thin layer of soil. Like jewels strewn at our feet, we are in country that provides a feast for rock enthusiasts.

Three sets of Rocky Mountains have uplifted, eroded, and determined the land, geologists believe today. We can see them all. The original, four hundred million years ago, wore away, creating the red-layered hills across the road. The next appeared sixty-five million years ago, and the most recent five million years ago, with five thousand feet of relief, providing the mountains behind us.

Three sets of Rocky Mountains uplifted and eroded—all visible to the naked eye.

But how they were formed remains a matter of conjecture. "The Rockies are poorly understood," Gregg says. "I can tell you how the Himalayas were formed, when India smashed into Asia. Or, how the Appalachians were formed, when Africa crashed into North America. Most mountain ranges are formed by huge landmasses crashing together. The Rockies were not. Perhaps, because the Earth's mantle is so thin here, that when tectonic plates shifted, this land buckled. It's hard to know."

Nature keeps a few secrets. After all, geologic time comes in millions and billions of years. Still, many of nature's secrets are revealed through rocks, like pages from a cosmic diary. Rocks relate stories about the stress and strain on our planet. The language appears as erosion or fault lines or deposited sediment. Colorado will tell some stories so clearly that even the naked eye can read between the lines.

Gregg points out a rock formation called joints, which results from freezing.

ROCKS REVEAL EARTH'S HISTORY

At our feet is a hill of igneous rock, smooth domes covered by green and gray lichen with flecks of orange lichen. "Granite," Gregg says, "and like all igneous rock, in a molten state at one time." This pink granite is called Silver Plume, believed to be 1.4 billion years old. Once, it was deep below the surface, but erosion wore away any soil and we sit on the exposed granite domes.

Basic geology is simple. Every rock in the world falls into one of three groups. First, there's igneous, which, like our pinkish granite, was originally molten, like lava or basalt. Then there's sedimentary, sandwiched clay and sand, which makes up the ancestral sandstone Rockies across the highway. The third is called metamorphic, midway between the first two. It's any rock that has been buried and subjected to such high temperatures and pressure that crystals form. Marble, quartzite, gneiss, and schist fall into the last category. All can be found in Colorado, and many are mined.

Mountain mahogany bushes sprout from the granite hill we stand on. It's an isolated swath of greenery in a sea of short prairie grasses. Our small island of

Tiny magenta garnets run through a white quartz ribbon in a metamorphic rock.

shrubbery exists, Gregg says, because water lingers for the seeds of shrubs: "On the grasslands, the water sinks in too fast. Only fast-acting grass roots can take up that water. Here, the water is prevented from sinking too deeply into the soil by the rocks. That allows the shrubs and trees to have access to that water."

On our way to Phantom Canyon Preserve, Gregg stops at a ravine. We're standing on a fault line, he tells us in a serious tone. He suspects a curious scarp, or gash, in the earth may indicate the fault line is moving, causing stress and strain on the grassland surface. Another geologist, Adam, is curious. He walks toward the scarp and notices the indentation runs up the hill; we can see the slight depression in the grass. "Perhaps just a slope failure," Adam says, and the two puzzle over the arrival of new weeds in the ravine. They speculate on cracks found in a nearby dam. Perhaps two rods driven in the soil with a rope attached could measure the degree to which the earth is pulling away. Neither comes to a firm conclusion about the scarp. "Geology," Gregg says with a sigh, "is the science of ambiguity."

PHANTOM CANYON PRESERVE

We head down a slippery slope. On these 1,700 acres, a sheltered canyon has been set apart by The Nature Conservancy. Along with easement rights from neighboring ranchers, it is hoped it will provide habitat for animals as they are pushed off land destined for development.

It's also a canyon that provides rich fodder for naturalists in search of interesting rock formations. The rock-sided canyon is temptation enough for us. We step on plenty of igneous and sedimentary rocks until Gregg stops us at a metamorphic rock. It's filled with tiny magenta garnets that run through a white quartz ribbon "like raisins in a pudding," Gregg says. He labels the rock: a xenolith schist. Alongside is a shiny silver mica muscovite with its transparent layers peeling away.

Above our heads, someone catches a glimpse of a golden eagle. Unlike a turkey vulture, whose wings are bent in flight, the eagle's wings are straight. And although it's high above, we recognize that this raptor is large.

Golden eagles usually mate for life. The pair in the canyon produced no young this year, although they have in previous years. Their nest is an enormous collection of limbs, larger than a king-size bed. It's tucked into a small shelf etched on the steep canyon wall. Eagles rarely abandon a nest; they rebuild on top of an old nest. Since it looks bigger than a 1950s Cadillac, it's easy to see why. The task of construction could take a lifetime. Jennifer Abbott, the overseer of the reserve, says that someone once climbed up to this eagle's nest and extracted a limb from the bottom. "Carbon dating indicated it was five thousand years old," she says, suggesting that it has been recycled by generations of golden eagles.

We turn our gaze to the canyon walls, a flat surface made up of rocks that have fractured without falling. Long black streaks are called desert varnish. Manganese oxide streaks canyon walls in Moab, Utah, too. Water from the North Fork of the Cache la Poudre River has seeped and left its mineral

Long black streaks on the canyon walls are called desert varnish.

deposits on the rocks. Grooves like giant claw marks run down the sides. These are bands of metamorphic rock layers that alter the structure of the rock.

The river has eroded the valley, with one side smooth while the other is rocky. The smooth side is dirt from metamorphic rock that has sifted down a hillside and settled along a bank. The other side of the riverbank is rough igneous stone.

River and wind erosion are obvious, but we've not considered perhaps the most important form of erosion here. "Freezing water can shatter the biggest and strongest rocks," Gregg says about the canyon walls, "because water expands when it freezes. When rocks crack from pressure,

Phantom Canyon is one of the rare canyons with no road leading to it.

those cracks are called joints—those came after the rocks were made."

ELEMENTS AND MINERALS: BASIC BUILDING BLOCKS

Before rocks were made, there were minerals. And before minerals, came elements. Some elements, such as uranium or gold, look and feel like rocks. Two elements together become a compound, like quartz (silicon dioxide), which is embedded along with feldspar and other minerals into granite rocks.

Some minerals, like asbestos, also look and feel like rocks. Talc is a mineral, and so is a purple gemlike fluorite that is mined in Colorado for fluoride toothpaste. Gregg passes around samples of quartz crystals, gold and silver, shale with fossils of ferns, and silicon.

Much of Colorado history, often violent and tragic, has centered on Earth's basic building materials. A gold rush in Colorado was followed by a race for silver. The discovery of coal led to waves of European immigration, dangerous working conditions, and eventual labor strife. Asbestos caused lung disease among the miners. Uranium built the atomic bomb. Silicon remains the basic element of a computer chip today.

But on a summer day, with storm clouds rolling in, rocks tell a different story, independent of human intervention. Water, wind, and cold temperatures continue to sculpt valleys. As we crouch at the bottom of the canyon, lightning is bouncing off the ridges. Weather may be the most dynamic factor in altering the land, but the basic materials have gained our respect. Rocks are appreciated as canyons or mountains, or treasure. But the real value is rarely understood. Rocks shape land forever, altering who and what can survive. "Landscape is determined by rocks," Gregg says, "if you know what to look for."

RESOURCES

■ COLORADO GEOLOGY

Black Canyon of the Gunnison National Park, 102 Elk Creek, Gunnison, 81230; 970-641-2337 or 970-641-2337, ext 205; www.nps.gov/blca.

Colorado National Monument, Fruita, 81521; 970-858-3617; www.nps.gov/colm. See additional geology field notes at www.aqd.nps.gov/grd/parks/colm.

Friends of Dinosaur Ridge, 16831 West Alameda Parkway, Morrison, 80465; 303-697-3466; www.dinoridge.org. Offers guided tours of the geology and paleontology of Dinosaur Ridge.

■ HELPFUL ORGANIZATIONS

Colorado Geological Survey, 1313 Sherman Street, Room 715, Denver, 80203; 303-866-2611; http://geosurvey.state.co.us.

The Colorado Nature Conservancy, 2424 Spruce Street, Boulder, 80302; 303-444-2950; http://nature.org/states/colorado.

Colorado School of Mines, Geology Museum, 1516 Illinois Street, Golden, 80401; 303-273-3815; www.mines.edu/Academic/geology/museum.

Colorado State Archives, 1313 Sherman Street, Room 1B-20, Denver, 80203; 303-866-2358; www.archives.state.co.us/arcgeog.html. State geography.

Denver Museum of Nature & Science, 2001 Colorado Boulevard, Denver, 80205; 303-322-7009; www.dmns.org.

■ RECOMMENDED READING

Hiking Colorado's Geology by Ralph Lee Hopkins and Lindy Birkel Hopkins (The Mountaineers, 2000). Guide for backpacking and hiking rock-enthusiasts.

Minerals of the World by C. A. Sorrell (Golden Guide to Rocks and Minerals, 1974).

The Practical Geologist: The Introductory Guide to the Basics of Geology and to Collecting and Identifying Rocks by Dougal Dixon and edited by Raymond I. Bernor (Simon & Schuster, 1992). Collecting and identifying rocks; goes into depth.

Roadside Geology of Colorado, Second Edition, by Halka Chronic and Felicie Williams (Mountain Press Publishing, 1980). Best everyday guide; can be used by motorists.

Basin and Range by John McPhee (Noonday Press, 1990).

■ WEBSITES

Touring Colorado Geology; www.geocities.com/jghist. Online tour of Colorado rocks, fossils, and stratigraphy.

■ Birding at Barr Lake: A Peaceable Kingdom of Feathered Friends

by NIKI HAYDEN

Even if you didn't know that Barr Lake is a premier Colorado spot for bird-watching, in a quick visit you'd soon find out. For the unacquainted, Barr Lake is surrounded by giant cottonwoods and willows, which house hundreds of birds. The closer you get, the louder the broadcasting of trills, caws, chirrups, whistles, and melodies. In an instant, you'll catch twenty bird songs floating through the air—signs of abundance in a habitat that once was a buffalo wallow. Now, it's a Colorado showpiece just outside Brighton.

Colorado State Parks ranger Mary Bonnell likens Barr Lake to an oasis for birds. "Out on the prairie there's not much unless you are a prairie bird. This is a suitable place to stop, get a bite to eat, and be safe—over three hundred fifty kinds of birds have been spotted here. For a lot of birds, the insect selection is great. A little bird like a warbler will find mosquitoes. If you are a duck, you don't have to worry about predation. And a bird of prey will find plenty of rodents."

A fisherman spears a carp with a bow and arrow.

MODERN-DAY SUCCESS STORY

In June, a small group of bird enthusiasts join longtime bird-watcher Lee Rowe for a slow meandering walk along the water's edge. Although Colorado is a semiarid region that periodically faces drought, Barr Lake has been spared the destructive ravages so far. A shrinking ditch on the dry side of our path makes minnows easy pickings for a killdeer. Its striking black and white neck rings, certain song, and familiar legs of a shorebird—thin storklike limbs—help for quick identification. In the distance, a western meadowlark sits high atop a dried mullein stalk, yodeling its remarkable trill. We can hear it singing loudly; it's much harder to spot the songster.

Barr Lake might be assumed to be the relic of an ancient bird retreat, but it's actually a contemporary environmental success story. Originally a buffalo wallow, the slight depression in the land collected rainfall several hundred years ago, and buffalo congregated to bathe luxuriously in the mud. The buffalo attracted Cheyenne and Arapaho hunters, who quickly recognized a place of destination for their hunting forays.

By the late nineteenth century, settlers realized that the depression could be dammed and provide a reservoir for clean water by diverting the South Platte River. But in the 1930s, Denver's sewage, dumped into the South Platte, filled Barr Lake, making it a huge cesspool. Then in 1965, two events saved the lake. Denver built a new sewage system and shortly after, a major flood cleaned out Barr Lake, providing clean water and a major stopover for birds of all kinds.

Lee Rowe adjusts his scope for bird-watching at Barr Lake.

"It's nearly two thousand acres of water when full," Mary says. "Then it gets drawn down for irrigation purposes, which creates more habitat because birds like to shop for lunch along the muddy banks. It's like a prairie pothole. When it dries up there are more insects to eat. And some, like the kingfisher birds, will capitalize on fish stranded in pools."

Diversity of Birds Makes the Lake a Destination

Lee stands poised, binoculars strung around his neck and scope slung over his shoulder, searching the trees for any signs of warblers. "I haven't seen any," he says with a sigh. Lee keeps an eye out for birds, noting down and relaying information to the state rangers. Some rangers have heard yellow warblers, which usually are hidden, searching for insects under leaves of a tree. This year some unusual birds have taken refuge at Barr Lake, blown in by storms or wind currents. A variety of warblers and cardinals now call Colorado home.

Where we stand, the trees are brimming with Bullock's orioles. They're easy to notice: the males sport bright orange heads and bodies offset by black markings; the females are nearly as impressive with chartreuse yellow heads and bellies. A flash of bright color identifies these birds that live along the ditches and rivers of Colorado. "The Bullock's oriole looks like it belongs in the Amazon," Mary says. "Their voices are wonderful, and once the cottonwoods lose their leaves, you can see their nest pouches made from grass fibers hanging from branches."

Above, a Swainson's hawk soars, the black and white speckled appearance neat as a pinstripe suit. Two grackles are following the hawk, squawking and nagging but not fearless enough to attack. The hawk soars, unimpressed by its detractors. Swainson's hawk is typical of many Barr Lake birds. After wintering in Argentina, the hawks make their way north, lured by the fish at the lake. Skillful hunters, they often find the catch of the day is taken from them by a magnificent bully on the block: a bald eagle.

Bald Eagles Reign

A male and female pair of bald eagles perches on a limb in the shade, just one tree away from their twelve-week-old fledglings. The two offspring stand on a nest that would fit a queen-size mattress—the frame a layer of branches, the inner nest filled with a softer straw. Peering through the scope reveals the two fledglings flapping their wings furiously and nearly ready to fly. They are entirely black and won't develop the white feathers that cover their parents' heads until fully grown.

There's only one bald eagle nest at Barr Lake. The lake is too small for another family because bald eagles require considerable territory. These parents chase off any eagles that dare to enter their space and do likewise with their own brood at the end of summer. Adult male and female partner for life until one dies or until they cease to produce viable eggs.

"When they are nesting they get territorial," Mary says, "but when the nesting season is over, you have a complement of eagles that come down to spend time in the winter. Last winter we saw twenty-two. Many are immature, so the old eagles will let them be. We stop seeing immature eagles in March, when the hatch happens."

The bald eagles, like the black-crowned night heron, the great blue heron, and the double-crested cormorant, have settled along the side of Barr Lake where boats are banned. They alone are allowed to fish. It's not only the water that draws the birds, but an abundance of stocked fish providing a plentiful feast.

CHANGES THROUGH THE YEARS

Throughout the years, some birds have swelled in number and others have diminished, Lee tells us. A few are rare and always a welcome sight. We catch an uncommonly viewed belted kingfisher in midair, the black fringed topknot an elaborate coiffure. Lee is elated.

The mammals have changed, too. Fox dens line up along the path, but there are no red foxes to inhabit them. They've been chased away by coyotes that find foxes unwanted competitors for any stranded or wounded birds on the ground.

At the water's edge we spy mallard ducks trailed by ducklings. A western grebe dives and stays down longer than we imagined possible. The courtship behavior of the grebe is famous. "With heads bobbing, they run across the top of the water," Mary says. "Side by side with wings outstretched, they look like ballet dancers."

Walk along the narrow boardwalks to bird blinds. That's where you'll be able to get a bit closer to the waterfowl. American white pelicans lounge on

As seen through a scope, a pair of bald eagle fledglings hovers on the edge of their giant nest.

small islands in the middle of the lake. They'll not venture to the shore's edge, we are told. These are bachelor herds; those who find a mate will choose a larger reservoir with islands set far away from any humans. Most of us link pelicans with the ocean, but these are usually landlocked, spread throughout Canada, Utah, Nevada, the Dakotas, and Minnesota.

A red-shirted fisherman is spearing carp with bow and arrows, his boat nestled into the weeds surrounding the lake. He takes careful aim but comes up empty. Few people will fish for carp, and it's the unusual bird that eats them.

A Peaceable Kingdom

Unlike the tundra of Rocky Mountain National Park where you'll find specialty birds, at Barr Lake, the rare and the ordinary mix freely. We spot the garden variety black-billed magpie, tree swallow, house finch, house wren, common grackle, and European starling. But we also catch an uncommon glimpse of the orchard oriole, and our guide quietly cheers.

The birds appear to tolerate each other in this tiny speck of paradise, but other encroachments loom. Although Denver International Airport is six miles away, the rangers haven't noticed much effect. More serious is the development of housing and shopping malls all around. What allows Barr Lake to thrive is a land buffer around the lake that provides shelter and native grasses for those birds that eat seeds or insects on prairie plants. And should Barr Lake be drained dry in a drought, farmers have first rights for the water. Rangers are hoping that both people and nature will cooperate.

Barr Lake is an oasis for migrating birds—
a chance to rest and catch a bite to eat.

Of course, a few birds are uncooperative themselves. Lee glowers at what appears to be a brown-headed cowbird, known for laying eggs in the nests of other birds, which then feed the babies to the detriment of their own brood. "Other birds are learning some coping measures for those cowbirds," Lee says. "Some build a new nest and lay new eggs; others have learned to recognize the cowbird egg and push it out of the nest." But on second viewing, it turns out to be a benign western kingbird.

Each morning, Mary, the daughter of an ornithologist, arrives at the lake and takes a front row seat. "I just close my eyes and hear the songs. You can hear twenty players in a symphony, and it changes every season. Even in winter you always hear the northern flickers and the black-capped chickadees. I can sit there and tell you what month it is. You know it's summer when you hear the warbler singing, 'Sweet, sweet, I'm so sweet.' And in winter Barr Lake is unbeatable for birds of prey. It's so primitive and stark, and then you'll see bald eagles and an accompaniment of red-tailed hawks and kestrels."

Across the gravel parking lot, a flapping feathered creature runs across the road. It's a reminder that some of the birds are prairie rather than water birds. Its ungainly jerky legs look stiff, as if arthritic joints prevent fluid movement, but it's only the stride of the ring-necked pheasant. A vivid red strip around its neck reveals this transplant from China. Originally imported as game birds, we claim them now as our own. In the fall, their voices can be heard in the tall grasses, along with the *swish-swish* sounds of the coyotes, equally invisible. And while few rangers actually see either of them once the grasses are at their peak, the noises and voices continue through the autumn.

RESOURCES

■ DIRECTIONS

From Denver, take Interstate 76 northeast. Exit on Bromley Lane; go east to Piccadilly Road, then south to the park entrance.

■ GENERAL INFORMATION

Barr Lake State Park, 13401 Piccadilly Road, Brighton, 80603; 303-659-6005; www.parks.state.co.us. One-day entrance fee is $5.

■ HELPFUL ORGANIZATIONS

Audubon Colorado, 3107B Twenty-eighth Street, Boulder, 80301; 303-415-0130; www.auduboncolorado.org. Has numerous local affiliates. For excellent page of related links, go to www.auduboncolorado.org/birds.htm.

Colorado Bird Observatory, c/o Scott Gillihan, 14500 Lark Bunting Lane, Brighton, 80603; 303-659-4348; www.rmbo.org. Observatory is adjacent to Barr Lake.

Denver Field Ornithologists, Zoology Department, Denver Museum of Nature and Science, 2001 Colorado Boulevard, Denver, 80205; www.geocities.com/dfobirders. Their Rare Bird Alert can be reached at 303-424-2144.

■ RECOMMENDED READING

A Birder's Guide to Colorado by Harold R. Holt (American Birding Association, 1997).

The Guide to Colorado Birds by Mary Taylor Gray (Westcliffe Publishers, 1998).

AUTUMN

■ Strawberry Hot Springs: A Perfect Combination of Nurture and Nature

by BETH KRODEL

Not quite warm enough for water sports. Not nearly cool enough to hit the ski slopes. But September and October are the perfect months to make a weekend trip to one of Colorado's many inviting hot springs.

Steam evaporates from hot rocks at the entrance to Strawberry Hot Springs.

The state is home to hundreds of the bubbling baths—if you count every trickle and seep. About ninety-three of them are large enough to hold you and a few friends. But of those, only a few dozen are open to the public.

In my six years in Colorado, I've been to a dozen or so, including Mount Princeton, Glenwood Springs, Hot Sulphur Springs, and Eldorado Springs. But none has pleased me quite like the rustic elegance of Strawberry Hot Springs just northeast of Steamboat Springs.

Situated in an aspen-studded mountain valley in Routt National Forest, Strawberry's three sculpted pools offer the perfect mixture of nature and nurture. It's hard to say which is more soothing—the gorgeous views or the warm water.

The source of the pools is a series of hot springs that spew from the hillside at temperatures of about 150 degrees and flow into a cool mountain creek. The largest hot pool is kept at about 104 degrees; the smaller hot pool is about 102 degrees. The third pool can be frighteningly cold in my opinion, but many bathers enjoy the sharp contrast between hot and cold and say that it helps their circulation. One thing is for certain, if you soak in any of the pools long enough, you're bound to see wildlife—a deer, a rabbit, a fox, or one of the many species of bird.

Strawberry Springs: Rustic and Remote

Unlike many commercial hot springs, Strawberry offers a truly rustic experience. While Hot Sulphur Springs and Salida Hot Springs Aquatic Center offer changing rooms that are air conditioned and heated, Strawberry guests use a dirt-floor tepee for privacy when slipping on their swimsuits. And unlike Glenwood Springs and Indian Springs Resort, both of which are right along Interstate 70, Strawberry is far from the hustle and bustle of highways and city lights.

In fact, Strawberry is downright remote. The eight-mile winding dirt road from Steamboat to Strawberry is so hairy that four-wheel-drive vehicles are required in the winter, and any inexperienced winter driver who gets a vehicle stuck on the road gets a $500 fine. (Don't worry, two shuttle services run year-round between Steamboat and the hot springs.)

My first visit to Strawberry was in October 2000. My boyfriend, Bryan, and I were visiting his cousins who live just northwest of Steamboat. They suggested we borrow their mountain bikes and take a ride up to the springs on the Mad Creek Trail. It was a challenging hour-and-a-half ride—all uphill. And I was more than glad to be rewarded by Strawberry's soothing steamy water. I remember finding comfort in the sound of the small waterfalls that connected one rock-

Three pools, ranging from cool to moderately hot, offer temperature changes from winter to summer.

walled pool to another. And I remember stroking my sore feet along the sandy pool bottoms.

A Quiet Interlude

Bryan, who had been to Strawberry many times a decade ago while he was a snowboard bum in Steamboat, recounted stories of raucous parties at the hot springs. I couldn't help but be thankful that the current owners had gone out of their way to curb obnoxious behavior. It was hard for me to imagine this soothing place as anything but serene. Even the small children played quietly in the warm water.

Since that first trip, we've made several. We usually try to pair the relaxing experience with some sort of athletic endeavor. We have made our way to the

springs not only on mountain bikes, but also on foot and on snowshoe. And each time, it has been worth the trip.

We've been there early enough to see the morning mist vanish with the sun and late enough to gaze at the evening stars, but we've never spent the night—in part because we've always had a free place to stay in town. But for those looking to immerse themselves in the Strawberry experience, rustic cabins and camping spots are available.

Boulder resident Rob Krissel stumbled across the Strawberry Hot Springs cabins on the web while searching for campgrounds in the Steamboat area. "I picked it because I thought it would be something different," says the thirty-two year old, who was planning a weekend trip for himself and four friends running the Steamboat Marathon and Half Marathon.

A thick forest of pines provides privacy with a cluster of chairs beckoning guests to the pool's edge.

Krissel, whose group of five paid $16 per person per night, says he highly recommends the overnight experience: "The scenery is beautiful, the pools are huge, and it's not too expensive." But he cautions that it might not be for everyone. "It's definitely rustic—just a couple of beds and a gas stove," he says. "But that's what I really liked about it."

That and the hot springs, of course. And the cost of admission to the springs is included in the lodging fees.

For those not spending the night, entry is $10 for adults on weekends and $5 for adults on weekdays. In her book *Colorado's Hot Springs,* Deborah Frazier George calls hot springs "the last recreation bargain in a state of $55 ski lift tickets, $20 passes to amusement parks, and $10 parking tabs for professional sports."

Some bathers believe in the healing powers of springs.

It's an especially good deal if you consider that a visit to hot springs is more than just recreation. Many bathers today, like the Ute Indians centuries before them, believe that the springs have medicinal powers—powers over disease and even death.

Although I was unable to find any scientific research to support these age-old claims, I can at least say that the combination of the soothing water and the beautiful setting of Strawberry Hot Springs relaxes my mind and body in a way that no Jacuzzi ever has.

RESOURCES

■ DIRECTIONS

Take U.S. Route 40 (Lincoln Avenue) west through Steamboat Springs. Turn right (northeast) on to Seventh Street. Go through a residential neighborhood and turn left (north) on to Park Road. Continue north on the dirt road for eight miles.

■ GENERAL INFORMATION

Strawberry Hot Springs, 44200 County Road 36, Steamboat Springs, 80487; 970-879-0342; www.strawberryhotsprings.com. Information on lodging, reservations, what to bring, private parties, and other services such as Watsu (warm-water massage).

■ SHUTTLES FROM STEAMBOAT

Strawberry Park Hot Springs Tours, Gondola Square, Steamboat Springs, 80487; 970-879-1873 or 800-748-1642.

Sweet Peas Tour, 850 Weiss Drive, Steamboat Springs, 80487; 970-879-5820.

■ RECOMMENDED READING

Colorado's Hot Springs, Second Edition, by Deborah Frazier George (Pruett Publishing, 2000).

■ OTHER HOT SPRINGS

In case the Strawberry Hot Springs are too remote for you, here's a list of other commercial hot springs near major roads and within a few hours' drive of the Front Range.

Historic Eldorado Springs Resort, 294 Artesian Drive, Eldorado Springs, 80025; 303-499-1316; www.eldoradosprings.com/about/eldo_spgs.html. Between Golden and Boulder, west of Colorado Highway 93 in Eldorado Canyon.

Hot Springs Lodge and Pool, 415 Sixth Street, P.O. Box 308, Glenwood Springs, 81601; 970-945-6571; www.hotspringspool.com.

Hot Sulphur Springs Resort and Spa, 5609 County Road 20, P.O. Box 275, Hot Sulphur Springs, 80451; 970-725-3306; http://hotsulphursprings.com. Just off of U.S. Route 40 between Granby and Steamboat Springs.

Indian Springs Resort, 302 Soda Creek Road, P.O. Box 1990, Idaho Springs, 80452; 303-989-6666; www.indianspringsresort.com.

The Springs Resort Hotel, P.O. Box 1799, Pagosa Springs, 81147; 970-264-4168 or 800-225-0934; www.pagosaspringsresort.com.

Yampah Spa and Salon, 709 East Sixth Street, Glenwood Springs, 81601; 970-945-0667; www.yampahspa.com.

■ JEWELS OF THE FOREST: HUNTING THE WILD MUSHROOM

by NIKI HAYDEN

With shiitake, oyster, wood ear, and portobello mushrooms in the stores, it's hard to judge the difference between a wild and cultivated mushroom. Here's the definition: wild mushrooms must be collected from the forest and cannot be cultivated on a mushroom farm. The exquisite, tender chanterelles or the robust, meaty boletus rarely are found fresh in stores. But they can be discovered in the mountains of Colorado.

Mushrooms may be found in abundance, but most, if not poisonous, are inedible. Only a few are delicious.

That's because most cultivated mushrooms grow on compost, like dead wood, while chanterelles grow at the roots of lodgepole pines. The boletus, also called porcini or cep, grows only among fir and spruce. "The trees cannot exist without their fungal partners," says Marilyn Shaw, a toxicologist for the Colorado Mycological Society, a group that studies mushrooms, "and the mushrooms cannot exist without their trees." Each shares nutrients, which are exchanged between the rootlets of both mushrooms and trees.

While there are thousands of mushrooms in Colorado, when it comes to culinary wild mushrooms, you'll find only a few delicious jewels of the forest that invite acclaim. Don't let the mix-up of names confuse you. For example, it may be called porcini in Italy, steinpilz in Germany, cep in France, or boletus in America. But all refer to a single species of a divine wild mushroom, *Boletus edulis.*

The Japanese adore the matsutake white mushroom *(Tricholoma magnivelare)*. The French swoon over the chanterelle *(Cantharellus cibarius)*, comparing its scent to the ripe aroma of apricots. There's the shaggy man mushroom, also known as the lawyer's wig. You'll also find the oyster mushroom *(Pleurotus ostreatus)*.

Mushrooms may change remarkably according to their maturity, so look to an expert who can identify all stages.

The lobster mushroom *(Hypomyces lactifluorum)*, exactly the color of a lobster's shell, is a parasite fungus that attacks another mushroom, replacing one fungus with another until there is not a bit of the original mushroom left.

Big puffballs are a favorite for some, while others yearn for a fresh morel as the first taste of spring. Any of these mushrooms may be essential to a particular cuisine, whether it's Chinese, Japanese, or French. But they all have one thing in common—you can find them in Colorado. Spring is the season for morels, while chanterelles and boletus are best dug in August.

The End of the Season

On a damp, chilly day in September, Andree Nino sets off for a mushroom foray not far from her ski cabin in Winter Park. As a child, Andree hunted wild

The lobster mushroom turns a beautiful shade of red from a parasite fungus that attacks the original mushroom.

mushrooms in France with her father and brother. They harvested chanterelles and boletus each summer. Her mother simmered the chanterelles in cream; boletus were sliced and sautéed in olive oil for omelettes. To her great surprise, Andree walked along the foot of the mountain behind her cabin and found the same mushrooms she remembered as a child.

But on this day, the season is waning and we're finding russula mushrooms—only barely edible and not at all tasty. Squirrels love them, and they provide a plentiful food source through the winter for wildlife. We turn over a small mound of earth and discover a kind of truffle—but not of the culinary species. Our brown, uninteresting truffle is cut in half and has only a musty, acrid taste on the tongue. In one instance, we think we have found a matsutake, the flavorful mushroom so beloved in Japanese cuisine. A good specimen could be sold for up to $100 in Japan. But ours is only an overgrown russula.

We're contemplating what we will cook if we can find the fungi we prize: "I like to cut up the boletus and sauté it in olive oil with garlic and parsley. But the chanterelles have a more delicate flavor," Andree says. "I just sauté them in a little butter and add some crème fraîche. You don't want to drown the wonderful flavor of those mushrooms."

Another mushroom she loves, the hawk's wing *(Hydnum imbricatum),* has proved more elusive for her. That's because each year, the harvest of mushrooms differs. Trying to determine exactly why a plentiful crop one year should dwindle the next isn't easy. Rainfall and temperature are not the only factors.

The oyster mushroom grows in white layers on dead wood.

Marilyn has noticed that mushrooms are more abundant when they are under stress. "If the weather is hot and dry, then suddenly there's plentiful rainfall, you'll get a banner crop of mushrooms. Morels will fruit more after a forest fire," she says, "and others will spread quickly over disturbed ground." It's as if the mushrooms suspect they are in danger and must multiply to escape extinction.

This large porcini was a prize specimen at the Colorado Mycological Society.

In other years, the mushroom spores can remain dormant season after season.

IDENTIFYING WILD MUSHROOMS

To identify a mushroom, it helps to inspect it in all stages, "the young, the mature, and the declining," Marilyn says. "It's not wise to identify mushrooms by picture matching, because people photograph the best specimens, so a lot of [the] time what you are finding will not be that pristine. Every once in a while you'll hear that even the experts get sick. We don't. We don't eat mushrooms if we don't know the identification." For beginners, it is recommended to go on a foray with an expert who will point out exactly what you need to look for.

The lore around mushrooms suggests that poisonous fungi can rub off on your hands. Once your hands touch your lips, you'll faint in a deadly swoon. That's not true. Only a few wild mushrooms are deadly, and many won't kill you but will make you ill. Some are hallucinogenic. The one that Alice ate in *Alice in Wonderland* is thought to be an iridescent red with glittery silver or white specks. In real life, it's called the *Amanita muscaria* and is frequently found in literature and folklore. Marilyn says that in Siberia it serves as a substitute for alcohol among the older generation. The effects of ingestion are more like inebriation than those of a true hallucinogen.

Somehow the *Amanita muscaria* in Siberia is not as toxic as the same mushroom found here. The North American *Amanita* also causes inebriation, but it's

Difficult to find and particularly savored in Japanese food is the matsutake mushroom.

accompanied by vomiting and severe intestinal distress.

Whether you cook wild or cultivated mushrooms, each shares common characteristics. They are at least 95 percent water, so it's advisable to sauté them slowly, which releases much of their water and concentrates the flavor. Mushrooms should not be eaten raw; they contain carcinogens that can be muted by cooking. Each mushroom varies in its nutrients, but all contain protein and trace minerals.

Chanterelles, among the most delicate and prized, are associated with French cuisine.

"Tomatoes, cheese, and mushrooms have a somewhat meatlike taste," says Christine Stamm, who teaches culinary classes at Johnson & Wales University in Denver. Wild mushrooms substitute for meat in the cuisine of Italy, where the boletus (porcini) is flavorful enough to top pasta. Boletus dries well and can be stored for years in a glass jar. Christine likes to whirl the dried boletus in a blender until it's nearly pulverized. Throughout the winter she adds several teaspoons to soups, stews, and sauces.

Mostly, mushrooms are prized for the extraordinary flavor they provide. "Wild mushrooms have lots of different flavors and textures," Marilyn says, "like the variety you would find in fruits and vegetables."

RESOURCES

■ HELPFUL ORGANIZATIONS

The Colorado Mycological Society, P.O. Box 9621, Denver, 80209; www.cmsweb.org.

Fungophile, P.O. Box 480503, Denver, 80248; 303-296-9359; www.shroomfestival.com.
Sponsors a Telluride mushroom festival each year in August. Offers field trips and classes for beginners and experts. The website is simply the town, now. A link to the festival can be found on the main website.

■ RECOMMENDED READING

Mushrooms of Colorado and the Southern Rocky Mountains by Vera Stucky Evenson (Westcliffe Publishers, 1997).

■ Splendor in the Grasses: Colorado's Prairie

by NIKI HAYDEN

Spring wildflowers are the prima ballerinas of nature. Showy and aromatic, each bloom beckons, enticing a bee or butterfly. But by late summer, the ballet corps—those stalwart grasses—pirouette on their own. With unremarkable flowers held aloft, they need only catch a slight breeze to continue their species.

Grasses take second place to wildflowers until the end of summer when their gold and red shines.

Bright yellow pollen hangs like tiny gold coins from grass stamens in September. You won't notice unless you look closely—too closely for those with an allergy.

"Just like a flower has an ovary and stamens, grasses are the same. The stamens are dangling and blow the pollen to the female stigmas. Grasses produce a lot of pollen, and that's why people who are allergic hate them," says naturalist Ann Cooper, who writes children's books about the worlds of science and nature.

A broad-brimmed hat protects her strawberry blond hair and porcelain complexion from the Colorado sun. A slight British accent reveals her origins. Although she has lived here nearly forty years, Ann examines Colorado with the enthusiasm of a newcomer.

"You can't really go back to where you came from," she says. "It's all changed. And in your new society, you're always a little set apart. That's what it is to be an immigrant. But I love the American idea of a melting pot."

What's left of the American prairie has become a horticultural melting pot. Ann points out that you'll rarely see the prairie as it originally existed. More wildflowers coexisted with the native grasses two hundred years ago. Once the prairie was plowed, the soil changed forever. Invasive grasses like smooth brome and cheatgrass bully their neighbors. Hay grasses, the elegant timothy and orchard, adapted and stayed. Cattle forage was planted years ago to combat erosion even in areas where cattle didn't graze. It's still planted in areas where livestock thrives. But closer to the foothills, plant ecologists try to reintroduce native species. One

Remnants of the tallgrass prairie survive in isolated pockets mixed with vigorous newly introduced agricultural grasses.

original native, Indian grass, is Ann's favorite and in top form come late summer. A red and ochre sheaf stands tall among other grasses. Indian grass is elegant and provides a swath of red in a meadow of golden grasses.

REMNANTS OF THE PRAIRIE

We're lucky to have found a healthy sea of grass. During an unusually hot and dry summer, many of the foothills and mountain flowers shriveled, forcing

The short-grass prairie reveals a wider selection of plants.

hummingbirds to fly to lower altitudes earlier than usual. Ann shakes her head at the scorched acres that usually sport spectacular specimens of big bluestem and Indian grass. In a marshy lot near a creek side, grasses have fared better.

"Big bluestem as tall as a man—well, almost," she quotes from a pioneer description that describes a man on horseback swallowed whole by tall prairie grasses. The stamens of blue grama grass, with their feathery spikelets, are labeled "grandmother's eyelashes."

Like native cottonwood trees, tallgrass prairie can be found only in areas with ample water.

Bluestem can go dormant in a dry spell; its deep roots will spread out as long as eight feet. If they can't go straight down in rocky soil like ours, they'll grow sideways. Blue grama, designated the official state grass of Colorado, grows in elegant bunches, its eyelash-shaped flower held high.

There's cordgrass with sharp sawtooth edges that scrape across bare legs. The tall grasses are sprinkled among smooth asters, goldenrod, showy milkweed, and wild alfalfa. Narrowleaf and plains cottonwoods cluster by a stream. They surround a native hawthorn, whose long slender thorns and berries make it a favorite hiding place for small birds seeking shelter from a hawk in search of dinner. Cottonwoods are a sign that these grasses get plenty of water; without water, cottonwoods wouldn't thrive. They're prairie trees, but only where they can dip their roots into streams.

Colorado once was a grand prairie that smacked into the mountains. Ann says pockets have survived—if you can find them. The Pawnee National Grassland and the Comanche Grassland, remnants of short-grass prairie, once were homesteads. Farmers found them too rocky to be plowed and sold the land back to the government. Closer to the foothills, where rainfall is more plentiful, tall prairie grasses thrive.

The switchgrass is nestled among the fringe sage and wild carrot. A shorter, delicate June grass shows off dried seed heads. We're walking into a transitional prairie zone where little bluestem and

Tallgrass prairie grasses obscure wildflowers.

sideoats grama alongside needle-and-thread grass remind us that we're in a mixed habitat of midsize grasses. Wild buckwheat arches tall. Small wild roses are covered in cherry red rose hips and threadleaf groundsel with bright yellow blossoms is in full bloom. Needle-and-thread grass is mixed with tall evening primrose.

"Grasses are determined by the rainfall," she says. "We have stranded relics of populations of tall grass. Switchgrass is a tall grass that will grow along an irrigation ditch. And where there are rock outcroppings toward eastern Colorado, where rain collects, you'll find medium-grass prairie. Rocky outcroppings also haven't been plowed or hayed, so you'll find original grasses."

Big bluestem boasts a burgundy stalk in September. Indian grass stands out with its golden red sheaf. Switchgrass sends delicate arching spikelets that dance in the breeze. A few blue chicory flowers, purple asters, and yellow mullein add spots of color. A colony of one grass ends where another begins. When the wind kicks up, the grasses make their own rustling music.

Indian grass *(Sorghastrum avenaceum nutans)*, with its handsome red and gold markings, adds an elegant swath of color.

The closer we move to the short-grass prairie, the more varied plants we'll find. It's as if the drier conditions have invited more guests to a limited feast. Dwarf leadplant, buffalo grass, and a variety of sunflowers show up. Snakeweed, a delicate yellow cluster of flowers, adds color, as does the nectar-rich native gayfeather. Each is covered in small bees and flies.

Grasses that have been overlooked in the past are popular with gardeners today. Little bluestem and switchgrass can be found in garden centers. Suddenly the textures and soft reds and golds in autumn colors are in fashion.

Buffalo grass and blue grama are touted by horticulturists for their drought-tolerant properties. And landscape architects sprinkle wildflowers among their grass gardens.

Grasses create a garden of their own, of sound and sway. Their stamina, modesty, and soft beauty have won us over.

RESOURCES

■ COLORADO PRAIRIE AND PRAIRIE GRASSES

Boulder Open Space and Mountain Parks, 66 South Cherryvale Road, P.O. Box 791, Boulder, 80306; 303-441-3440; www.ci.boulder.co.us/openspace. Pockets of ancient tallgrass prairie still remain in the foothills of Boulder. Check the Bobolink Trail and the South Boulder Creek Trail. Guided hikes available.

Comanche National Grassland, 27162 U.S. Highway 287, P.O. Box 127, Springfield, 81073; 719-523-6591; www.fs.fed.us/r2/psicc/coma. Short-grass prairie.

Denver Botanic Gardens, 1005 York Street, Denver, 80206; 720-865-3500; www.denverbotanicgardens.org. Both tallgrass and short-grass prairie gardens.

Pawnee National Grassland, Administrative Office, 660 O Street, Greeley, 80631; 970-353-5004; www.fs.fed.us/arnf/districts/png.

Rocky Mountain Arsenal National Wildlife Refuge, 56th Avenue and Havana Street, Building 121, Commerce City, 80022; 303-289-0232; http://rockymountainarsenal.fws.gov.

Up, Up, and Away: In the Belly of the Balloon

by BETH KRODEL

It's 5 A.M. on a Sunday, and the alarm clock is blaring its annoying beep. Bryan and I feel around the tent for clothes and socks, climb out of our sleeping bags, get dressed, and, still half-asleep, head for the car.

It's a thirty-minute drive from our campsite south of Minturn to the launch area in Edwards, just west of Vail, and we're supposed to be there at 5:45 A.M. The woman on the phone said we had to take off early in the morning while the wind is still calm.

We get to the launch area on time. No balloon in sight. They're about a half hour late. I'm not in a great mood, knowing I could have slept another thirty minutes.

But as Ed VandeHoef, owner of Broomfield-based Aero-Cruise Balloon Adventures, and his crew chief Chip Connolly start unloading the big brown basket and unrolling yard after yard of the multicolored balloon, I seem to forget my grumpiness.

Autumn is the most popular time to sail over the Rockies in a balloon.

There are ten of us at the launch area, including Ed and Chip, and I'm wondering how we're all going to fit in that woven basket. But we soon find out that only five of us will be ballooning—Ed will be piloting, and my friend Bryan and I will be joining John and Alice from Merriam Woods, Missouri, as passengers. Chip will stay on the ground to "chase" the balloon—coming to rescue us wherever we might land. The other four people, the Gorsuch family from Broomfield, were just along to watch. They had given the ballooning trip to their parents, John and Alice, as a thirty-ninth wedding anniversary gift.

Bryan and John hold open the mouth of the balloon, while Ed fills it with hot air. Chip spreads the polyester material across the ground and makes sure that it fills evenly.

Twenty minutes later, the balloon is fully inflated. We snap a few pix, and then the five of us pile into the basket. Just before taking off, Ed gives us a quick tutorial on what to do in case of a "high-wind landing." We're supposed to hold on tight and bend our knees, keeping all limbs inside the basket so that they don't get ripped off if the basket drags along the ground.

A balloon is inflated on its side.

Sailing Past Farms and Cities

OK. Now I'm a little scared. But off we go anyway. Ed gives the blast valve a few squeezes, releasing enough propane to send flames shooting into the mouth of the balloon just above our heads. We can feel the heat on our scalps.

At first, we climb slowly over a bright green farm just south of Interstate 70. The cows begin to get smaller and smaller, and the balloon shifts north across the highway, where cars whiz past underneath us. It's then that I notice our shadow against the ground—such an amazing sight. We float over a golf course and notice the interesting shapes of sand traps, and over residential neighborhoods, where even the patterns of houses and driveways look like abstract paintings.

After getting over the initial excitement, we begin drilling Ed about his credentials. He has been piloting hot air balloons for twenty-two years. He received his license in 1978 after going through a rigorous licensing process that included flight instruction, a written test, and a practical test given by a Federal Aviation Administration–designated examiner. We all feel reassured. Then, oops. It looks like we're headed straight for some trees. Butterflies start churning in my stomach. The entire basket is well below tree line, and the trees are approaching rapidly. Ed is smiling, but it makes me nervous that he isn't pressing the lever to shoot up more flames and lift the balloon. The trees keep getting closer.

Bright colors dot the landscape as balloons take off.

Finally, Ed makes flames, and the balloon lifts just in time. The basket barely clears the treetops. And then we're over a river. Ed maneuvers the balloon right down to the surface of the rushing water. We all ooh and ahh at its beauty.

An Easy Landing

For another hour, Ed pilots the balloon east and west across the Vail Valley with the New York mountain range to the south.

Around 9 A.M., he begins to look for a landing spot. We spot Chip following us in the truck. The wind pushes us past our launch area and it looks like we're heading for a neighborhood. There's an open road we could land in, but Ed said the neighbors don't like it when balloons tie up their street, so he pushes the balloon on farther up a hill.

No high-wind landing for us, thank goodness. Instead, it's just a light thud and a little bit of scooting across the ground. Each time a passenger climbs out, the balloon wants to lift off again, but Ed and Bryan pull with all their weight to keep it grounded.

Chip shows up with the truck, and we all get to help deflate the balloon and roll it up. It's fun to be a part of the entire experience, instead of just going along for the ride.

To experience a bird's-eye view is the best reason to sail over the landscape.

Once the balloon and basket are loaded, Ed tops off the morning with a simple breakfast of orange juice, champagne, and some of his mother's homemade zucchini bread with cream cheese. And he toasts us with the Balloonists' Prayer:

The winds have welcomed you with softness,
The sun has blessed you with its warm hands.
You have flown so high and so well that God
has joined you in your laughter,
And he has set you gently back into the loving
arms of Mother Earth.

Now it's your turn. With the annual changing of the color in the aspen leaves, it's a great time to schedule a hot-air ballooning adventure. "Most people think you have to have warm air to go up. They don't understand that ballooning is a year-round activity; you just have to dress accordingly," says Ed, pointing out that summer is his busiest season. "Really, the colder the better. If you have cold air on the outside of the balloon, you don't have to heat the inside nearly as much, so you can stay up longer. And you don't have to get up as early if you go in the fall or winter."

Ballooning is not an inexpensive outing. Most companies in Colorado charge $150 to $200 a person to ride with a small group.

But for people who love trying new things, it's well worth the money. And as John and Alice can attest, a balloon ride makes for a great gift. "Life is all about experiences," Alice says. "And this is one I'm glad to have had."

■ BALLOONING COMPANIES

Aero-Cruise Balloon Adventurers, 890 Hemlock Way, Broomfield, 80020; 800-373-1243 or
303-469-1243.

Big Horn Balloon Company, 14522 Mustang Lane, Montrose, 81401; 970-596-1008;
www.balloon-adventures.com/experience.html.

Camelot Balloons, P.O. Box 1896, Vail, 81658; 800-785-4743; www.camelotballoons.com.

Grand Adventure Balloon, P.O. Box 3423, Winter Park, 80482; 888-887-1340 or 970-887-1340;
www.grandadventureballoon.com.

Unicorn Balloon Company, 406 Aspen Airport business Center, Aspen, 81611; P.O. Box 38512,
Colorado Springs, 80937; 800-755-0935; www.unicornballoon.com.

Wild West Balloon Adventures, P.O. Box 882091, Steamboat Springs, 80488; 970-879-7219;
www.wildwestballooning.com.

■ BALLOON FESTIVAL

Colorado Springs Balloon Classic, 328 Bonfoy Avenue, Colorado Springs, 80909; 719-471-4833;
www.balloonclassic.com. Held at Memorial Park.

WINTER

■ More Than Meets the Eye: A Winter Walk in the Colorado Foothills

by NIKI HAYDEN

On a crisp, cold winter morning, naturalist Lynne Sullivan gathers her flock—a group of brightly coated hikers ambling along a Colorado mountain trail in search of wildlife. Lynne is a modern version of the old-fashioned ranger, a naturalist who guides others on mountain trails. Slender in the way that determined hikers often are, she wears layered clothing, thick-soled boots, and carries all the right stuff—water bottle and day-old pizza, sunglasses and binoculars.

A winter walk requires attention to subtle changes in nature.

Before setting off, we catch the strains of the noisy chickaree squirrel. We survey what looks like a winter stage before the performance, draped in a magnificent setting.

Some Are True Hibernators, Others Are Not

Our stage is empty so far. Black bears will be hidden in caves, slumbering in a state of torpor, a less intense form of hibernation than that of bats—the true hibernators. As we stride along a swath cut in the grasses, crevices and hidden overhangs could be the caves of bats, we suggest. But Lynne tells us that bats have headed farther up in elevation, the better to seek out a shelter that will not thaw during a sunny winter day. True hibernators, like bats, will die if they are warmed abruptly. Heat forces them to burn precious stored fat. Only the slow and steady thaw of spring allows their hearts to begin a gradual process of speeding up.

"They are one of the animals that goes into a higher altitude or a deep mine shaft because they are interested in a constant temperature. Even a small amount of heat can disturb them. One of the interesting tidbits about bats is that after mating, the sperm is stored by the female. It is only allowed to fertilize the egg after the bat leaves hibernation," Lynne says.

Of course, we are awestruck by this bit of information and wonder how biologists make such discoveries. But then, before we can fully appreciate bats, we're on to the birds.

A bird condominium consists of a dead tree with several holes for a variety of tenants.

BIRDS OUT AND ABOUT

Bats may be snugly tucked in, but birds are out and about. Dead trees, or snags, as Lynne calls them, are studded with holes for a variety of birds. We are ogling a bird condominium, one that mountain western bluebirds, nuthatches, American kestrels, and a few saw-whet owls will settle into. Above our heads a downy woodpecker with black and white body, capped by a vivid red patch on its head, taps along a dead branch.

Winter will change bird behavior. Summertime flocks may enjoy plentiful food and cover. In a group of Douglas fir trees, small birds swoop in formation. We barely hear their calls, but catch the quick movements of wings fluttering as they dart from tree to tree.

Smaller birds are dinner for birds of prey like the goshawk. To compensate, Lynne tells us, small birds have learned to help each other. Banding together like birds of a feather holds true. "It's called a mixed flock for birds. That's something that only happens in the winter. A chickadee can warn others about a goshawk or a Cooper's hawk.

Ranger Lynne Sullivan takes her brood on a walk.

When they warn each other, they are warning other birds as well." Also in winter, a mixed flock of small birds will elbow their way into territory dominated by larger birds. Ordinarily, they would never dare to take on the bigger bully birds.

A Forest of Douglas Fir and Ponderosa Pines

As we round a bend, the curve unveils a view of the Continental Divide. Snow-capped peaks in the distance host a formidable environment of

Clipped, small branches of ponderosa pine indicate the presence of Abert's squirrels.

alpine plants and treeless vistas. But where we stand, in the foothills of the Front Range, ponderosa pine trees and Douglas firs surround us. The pines shed their lower branches and develop a mop top shape. The Douglas firs maintain a perfect cone.

Ponderosa pines are drought-tolerant and will thrive on the sunny, dry south slopes of a mountain. Firs like water and grow thickly on the wetter, northern slopes.

On many of the branches, mistletoe has a lethal grip. Mistletoe is a parasite that rarely kills a tree, but will weaken it, allowing a more deadly enemy like the pine beetle to settle in. This particular mistletoe has only one chance to propagate. It must hurl seeds into the air with a force strong enough for it to catch on the limb of a neighboring tree. Mistletoe rarely gets a chance to take hold in a young forest where the trees are widely spaced, as ponderosas like to be.

But here, in a mature ponderosa forest where the trees have grown up and now form a dense canopy, mistletoe is found on many trees. As we

A variety of mistletoe that covers pine branches rarely makes lethal inroads except in a mature forest.

lament its grip on the forest, Lynne prefers to place mistletoe in a grander scheme: "We humans prefer pretty green forests, so we tend to look at this species as bad when, in fact, it is a protector of forest health."

SPECIALIZED RELATIONSHIPS ABOUND

Colorado is often called a region of microclimates. In this forest, ancient relationships between a few of the animals and plants serve to remind us of that truth. Take the Abert's squirrel. Not all animals will chew on the ponderosa pine. The mule deer, determined foragers, avoid them. But clipped needles on the ground indicate an Abert's is close by. These tiny squirrels don't bury nuts or cache food away for the winter. Instead, they clip off a branch and chew the fleshy inner bark.

But trees are not quiet victims of an Abert's hunger. They produce defenses. Ponderosa pines contain noxious chemicals called terpenes. "This is the basis for turpentine. The more terpenes a ponderosa produces, the less attractive it is to a squirrel. They will nest in one tree and eat in another, " Lynne says.

THE ELUSIVE MOUNTAIN LION

Mule deer are tasty meals to another animal—the secretive mountain lion. Lynne tells us that mountain lions once were found throughout much of North America. They sauntered on the Great Plains, crouching behind rock formations, feeding on mice or squirrels, and occasionally eating berries. Much of that territory and food has been lost to these big cats, but they're at home in the rocky ledges along

Firs take more water than ponderosa pines and can be found on wetter slopes.

The rocky outcroppings in the foothills are prime habitat for mountain lions.

the Front Range. The herds of deer provide abundant meals.

"They jump from rocks, preferring to be hiding and secretive in some location, pouncing on the prey rather than doing an elongated chase. Where you find their food source, you will find them. They may be in the cities more than we know, following waterways. But they don't run like a cheetah and prefer not to have to run a great distance," Lynne says. Sometimes you glimpse only a flash, but then their long tail swishes, giving them away.

We won't see any of these big cats; few people do. Instead, we glance over their domain—the rocky outcroppings—imagining their patient wait as unsuspecting deer stroll by.

When we round a corner along an icy patch, three long paw or claw marks have been etched in the snow. Perhaps they are the marks of the lion, scratching bits of debris together and urinating in the pile as a way of declaring territory. The marks are large, but slightly melted. We can't discern claw marks in the scratching, but our imaginations are at work, as if the big cat is ambling down our path at nightfall.

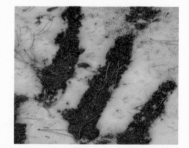

We imagine these big claw marks to be made by an elusive mountain lion.

INSECTS UNDER COVER

Around the bend, the vista opens again to the Continental Divide. Snow-capped mountains in the distance against a blue cloudless sky, we're in a sea of grass. Blue grama grass remains distinctive in winter with its eyelash-shaped tufts.

In the summer, Lynne says, spreading her hands out as if to take in the entire mountainside, the hill is filled with dragonflies. They fly up to feed on insects. But now they are nymphs, swimming in the icy streams and ponds. A few butterflies, like the mourning cloak, will winter over, clutching onto lichen-covered rocks. And ladybugs will journey up the mountains, producing a kind of anti-freeze as they ascend in elevation. "It's a thread of similar survival strategy that plants share with the animals, this making of alcohol for anti-freeze. Ultimately if temperatures plummet, they are trying to avoid a sharp ice crystal that will puncture a cell membrane," Lynne says.

THE BEGINNING OF SOIL

All along the hike we've passed lichen-covered rocks. These ancient combinations of fungi and algae link one of the simplest relationships. The fungi provide shelter, water, and minerals for the algae, which provide sugars and photosynthesis for the fungi. In a different environment perhaps each could live separately. But on this mountainside the combination is unbeatable. "These are extremely slow growing," Lynne says, "and can land on barren rock, where they start to grow. They are a pioneering organism. By that I mean that the lichen will excrete an acidic substance that breaks down the rock, turning that rock into soil."

Lichen helps to break down rocks into a gravel soil.

The consequences are obvious. Layers of lichen-covered rocks are crumbling, creating a sea of sharp pebbles called scree. As inhospitable as this gravel appears, it is the foundation for most mountain plants. Rocky Mountain penstemon and other natives thrive in scree patches.

It's fitting that we have come full circle around the mountain, and in nature, too. The end of our hike closes with the making of soil. Not the humus soil of the East Coast, or the deep earth of the Great Plains, but the

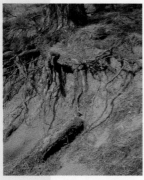
Under the harshest of conditions, some plants adapt to extremes.

thin soil of the Rocky Mountains, which allows only the toughest, best-adapted plants and animals to survive. "Look at that tree with its roots exposed," Lynne says. The ponderosa hugs an eroding hillside, determined to keep soil around its root ball as if it is covering something private and fragile. "It may be anthropomorphic, to equate people to trees," Lynne says, "but I like to think that nature is coping with stress, too."

RESOURCES

■ HELPFUL ORGANIZATIONS

Boulder Open Space and Mountain Parks, 66 South Cherryvale Road, P.O. Box 791, Boulder, 80306; 303-441-3440; www.ci.boulder.co.us/openspace. Guided hikes.

Colorado Mountain Club, 710 Tenth Street, Suite 200, Golden, 80401; 303-279-3080; www.cmc.org/cmc. Guided hikes.

Colorado State Parks, 1313 Sherman Street, No. 618, Denver, 80203; 303-866-3437; http://parks.state.co.us.

Wilderness Institute, University of Montana, School of Forestry, Main Hall, Room 307, Missoula, Montana 59812; 406-243-6933; www.wilderness.net.

■ RECOMMENDED READING

Colorado Nature Almanac: A Month-by-Month Guide to Wildlife & Wild Places by Stephen R. Jones and Ruth Carol Cushman (Pruett Publishing, 1998).

■ Moonstruck: Hiking by the Light of the Silvery Moon

by BETH KRODEL

Tired of the same old Saturday night routine—movies, dinner parties, watching TV at home? Why not get out under the stars with some friends and a thermos of hot chocolate and check out that celestial body that's been the topic of numerous songs, quotations, and myths.

The moon. *La luna.*

Full moons make for the perfect nighttime hiking. They offer enough illumination for you to see the trail and the beauty that surrounds you at a quiet time when few, if any, other hikers are out. And hiking at night gives you the chance to get a new perspective on your environment; you're likely to see animals that you don't during the day, and even some flora transforms at night, with blooms closing or leaves curling up.

Hiking at night reveals sounds and sights not caught in daytime.

My significant other and I organized two nighttime hikes recently: one under the full moon in October, the other during a meteor shower in November.

For the first hike, we headed to Brainard Lake just north of Nederland with twenty people and five dogs. Although it was only October, we made sure that everyone had gloves, hats, coats, and warm pants. And it turned out that we needed all of the above. It was extremely windy, and we even got a trace snow. Fortunately the reflection of the snow illuminated the trail even more.

We did a simple two-hour hike along the relatively flat Mitchell Lake Trail. Our guests, most of them in their twenties and thirties, were as giddy as little kids. "It's so invigorating," said Matthew Kear of Gunbarrel, who recently moved from Ohio to Colorado with his wife, Kate. "Doing things like this [is] part of why we moved out here." Christine Rause, who has lived in Boulder for ten years, was equally excited: "I can't believe I've never thought of doing this before. It's so gorgeous out. And it almost feels like we're doing something wrong since there's no one else around."

In fact, some hiking trails are closed at night, but others are open to anyone any time. Simply read the signs at the trailhead, or call the appropriate authority in advance to see if the trail you're interested in allows nighttime hiking.

You may not see any other hikers, so hike with companions.

IT'S JUST FOR FUN, SO PLAY IT SAFE

For our second adventure, we decided to pair the hike with a hearty meal—cornbread, chili, and all the fixings—just to help folks stay warm along the trail. This time, we had about a dozen people and dogs. And we chose a hike closer to home: Mount Sanitas in Boulder. Because we were concerned about ice deposits along the ridge, we hiked the gradually climbing valley trail. It wasn't a full moon, but the sky was clear, so we had a decent amount of light. And half of us brought headlamps.

Mount Sanitas can get quite steep near the summit, so we split into two groups—one that hiked to the top, another that stopped a little more than halfway up. Everyone agreed there was no need for anyone to feel uncomfortable or concerned about twisting an ankle. After all, we were there for the fun, the conversation, and the beauty. Our hike was during the Leonid meteor shower, and astronomers had predicted as many as one hundred meteors per hour that November. We saw only six, but they were beautiful, and we had a great time.

"It's amazing how peaceful it is out here at night," said Alicia Alpenfels, who sometimes walks her dog, Hudson, on the Sanitas Valley Trail during daylight hours. "During the day, you can't go ten feet without passing a person or a dog. And at night, you get all this," she said motioning toward the sky.

Even the most commonly hiked trails clear out by evening.

The good news for meteor watchers is that astronomers are calling for more Leonids in the future. David Asher of the Armagh Observatory in Ireland says, "Peak rates during those future years should reach at least ten thousand meteors per hour as Earth passes through debris trails from comet Tempel-Tuttle."

For more information on Leonids, full moons, and other neat astronomical phenomena, keep your eye on NASA's Astronomy Picture of the Day website at http://antwrp.gsfc.nasa.gov/apod. And start planning your hike today. Your friends will be surprised when you invite them for a night out on the trails instead of a night out on the town.

TIPS FOR NIGHTTIME HIKING

Dress appropriately. If you're going to higher altitudes, remember that a few thousand feet of elevation can mean a ten- to twenty-degree drop in temperature. And even in the summer months, it can be quite cold after sunset.

Bring water and/or something warm to drink. You should always keep yourself hydrated while hiking.

Go in a group. Simply put, it's safer.

Take a bell, or some other noisemaker. You may need something to scare away any unwanted wildlife such as mountain lions and bears. Check out the "What Do I Do" website from Boulder Mountain Parks:

www.ci.boulder.co.us/openspace/nature/lions_bears.htm.

Take at least one headlamp for every two people. Even if the moon seems especially bright, you never know when it might go behind a cloud.

Tell someone where you're going and what time you'll be back. This is an important precaution to take, just in case.

Check out any avalanche conditions before heading out (http://geosurvey.state.co.us/avalanche). Another potentially lifesaving precaution, and it only takes a moment.

RESOURCES

■ RECOMMENDED READING

365 Starry Nights: An Introduction to Astronomy for Every Night of the Year by Chet Raymo (Prentice-Hall, 1982).

■ WEBSITES

www.space.com. User-friendly site for amateur stargazers.

www.windows.ucar.edu. This wonderful website, designed by the University Corporation for Atmospheric Research, has extensive information on the moon and its relationship with the Earth.

■ GLIDING ON A BLANKET OF SNOW: SNOWSHOEING IN ROCKY MOUNTAIN NATIONAL PARK

by NIKI HAYDEN

The warnings were clear: lackluster snowfall, high winds, and icy conditions in Rocky Mountain National Park. But the lure was enticing—a snowshoe hike with a ranger for two hours of trails. For someone who has never donned a pair of snowshoes, the offer looked appealing. During the past four years, park rangers have collected would-be snowshoe enthusiasts for hikes during the winter months. "As boomers have aged," says ranger Susan Langdon, "they're looking for a less stressful way to get out in the wilderness. Less stress on their joints." Snowshoeing is as easy as walking, she says, as we soon will discover.

Snowshoeing has been embraced by a diverse group of winter hikers, from the intrepid to the timid.

The warnings have proved to be incorrect. No wind, a few snow flurries that we welcome, and while the snow is thin in spots, we discover plenty of fresh deep snow the higher we tread. On a Saturday morning, the parking lot at Bear Lake in RMNP fills quickly. Residents from the drought-stricken foothills are hungry for snow. Sleds, skis, snowshoes and ordinary hikers without snowshoes assemble at the trailheads. Our group numbers about twenty—from ten years of age to about sixty-five. Susan will lead the tour and volunteer ranger Dave Chambers stays behind to catch any strays. Our snowshoe walk is labeled beginner, but it will prove to be challenging for those who are unprepared for the altitude at 9,500 feet.

A Sport for all Ages

The hike is free after you've paid to enter the park. But you must make reservations. Since these hikes have become popular, the rangers will take

reservations no more than a week in advance. We've dressed in layers, brought sunscreen, sunglasses, snacks, and water. A few have purchased snowshoes, but most of us grabbed rentals in the town of Estes Park. Judging from the stores that rent snowshoes—from outdoor stores to bicycle shops—it's a popular sport. The stores know how to fit their customers and will offer tips on poles. The snowshoe is a basic and sturdy piece of equipment. On our hike, not a single individual complained about the shoes.

We set out on a hike that the ranger says will be half nature and half tips on the sport, or some might say, the leisure, of snowshoeing. Susan shows us how to get out of deep drifts, two techniques for going down a hill, how to use the poles correctly, and how to break

Our ranger tells us that Nymph Lake is frozen solidly and safe to glide across.

a new trail. Much of it is common sense, and perhaps what makes snowshoeing so compelling is that you don't have to think about technique. You just do it. Even the most inept look jaunty on a trail. As for athletic types—well, you can run in snowshoes, too.

When we set off at the trailhead of Bear Lake, the tips of the mountains are shrouded in mist. It's the mystical quality of the park that is one of its charms in winter. There's a sprinkling of snow that will come and go as the afternoon wears on and clouds above are moving at a rapid clip. Despite sudden and inexplicable

The ranger gives basic tips on how to snowshoe with ease.

Snowshoeing is not unlike hiking and is a great way to get around the snowy park.

weather changes in the park, our afternoon is perfect. Susan leads us through the trail, at first hard-packed with little need for snowshoes. Then she deviates into the woods where we are on a snowier trail. It has been cleared but retains the bounce of fresh snow.

From time to time, Susan stops to give us pointers on nature, allowing the slower ones among us to catch their breath. We're climbing a little over 200 feet and on the way, we'll hear some history of snowshoes—originally a Native American invention. Some are pointed in the back for snowshoe racing, we are told. Racing in snowshoes defies the quiet and patient rhythm that makes snowshoeing nearly a Zen experience. But we will see a few high-energy trekkers who bound through the woods like rabbits on steroids.

A Quiet Approach Brings Out Wildlife

Around a bend we chance upon a snowshoe hare, a rare encounter even for the experienced. "I haven't seen one in about four years," Dave exclaims. The hare sits perfectly camouflaged in a swale at the base of a pine. It's not just that the hare, being white, is the color of snow. But against the base of a tree, even his chocolate-colored eyes blend into the trunk's brown bark, and the hare's white fur is ringed by snow. Susan tells us that the winter white protects the hare from predators, but there's an additional benefit: the loss of color adds a pocket of air in the follicle shaft that will lend some insulation.

The hare will take our gawking for only so long and bounds away. His footprints leave distinctive marks in the snow, with the large feet planted ahead of

A snowshoe hare sits in the swale under a tree, nearly indistinguishable from snow.

his smaller front paws. He will feast on the calorie-rich pinecones that become available once snow piles under branches of the pines. Sleek and fat, this hare would be a tempting morsel for any of the park's coyotes or mountain lions.

A veil of mist hangs over the Rockies on a day that eventually turns sunny.

But the hare is not the only entrée on the menu for carnivores. Susan says there are hundreds of mice and voles under the snow at our feet. Coyotes will listen to the stirring sounds under the snow for their meals. The thin snow pack guarantees good hunting for coyotes because the voles' stirring movements will be easy for a clever coyote to hear.

More easily seen is a gray jay flitting from tree to tree. "Camp robber," Dave says about the eating habits of the bird. The jay's elegant gray coat with a black neck ring makes him look formal, as if he's on his way to a black-tie dinner.

Tree squirrels leap from tree to tree, "their transportation system," Susan says. Most animals don't hibernate in the winter. True, the bears are in a kind of torpor, where they sleep, squirm a bit, move around and sleep some more. But most animals, like the jays and tree squirrels, learn to cope with winter.

Understanding Nature's Dangers

Susan takes us to a trail that is covered by pristine snow. She tromps through and then, breathlessly, explains that it's a good idea to take turns breaking trail. We're then invited to dash into the snow ourselves and catch the exhilarating experience of new snow. Now it's easy to see why snowshoes were invented. Although you'll sink a bit, the shoes glide and keep our weight from plunging deeply, that is, until a small ponderosa pine snags a shoe, like a hook beneath the snow. "I need a friend," Susan says, and we pull her loose. "That's also why it's a good idea to be with another person," she adds.

We pass by Bear Lake, only a mist on the horizon to our eyes, but Susan points out the willow limbs. Willows, shrubby deciduous trees, grow only where water is plentiful. You'll find them at the base of mountains or ravines. Here, they ring a side of the lake. They serve as a warning, Susan explains, that water is nearby and to be wary of a lake that may not be frozen solid. Higher up, at Nymph Lake, we'll skate across a frozen lake.

Up, up we climb. We meet snowshoers and cross-country skiers, all destined to meet at Nymph Lake. In the summer, hikers head up to Dream Lake, too, but there's concern about avalanche danger at Dream Lake during the winter months. Susan points to the snow-faced rocks as perfect incubators for an avalanche. Colorado leads the nation in avalanche deaths, so she details the techniques to use should we ever find ourselves in one.

But that's not the major danger in the park. Dave's radio blares an accident report. A sled has crashed into a tree. Someone who radios a distress call suspects a possible fractured leg and hip. Soon a ranger has reached the victim and called for an ambulance. From far away, we hear the wail of a siren and we pass two rangers jogging to the scene with blankets in tow. When we return, a volunteer ranger will reveal that the sled accident is the second in nine days.

By the time we reach Nymph Lake, the icy wilderness opens to reveal peak after bald peak encased in snow. Like giant snow cones, the above-timberline rocky faces look heavily laden. The lake is only a few feet deep and solidly frozen, so it's safe to slide across as we head to the other side.

The ranger stands on the edge of a cornice, and, in a protective gesture, warns new snowshoers to slow down as they approach.

Downhill Brings Stunning Views

The rest of the trek is downhill and just around a bend we reach a cornice, or rocky ledge that overlooks the vast Bear Lake below. Susan warns us to slow down, that we'll reach the cornice quickly. Once there, the view is breathtaking, almost as if you can see the entire park in one vista.

New snow allows snowshoers to plow ahead and create a new trail.

Susan is perched at the edge, and as we 'ooh' and 'aah,' she tells us a little about Enos Mills, who left Kansas when he was fourteen and spent much of his life trying to create a national park in his beloved mountains. "He would climb a tree in a ferocious wind, the tree whipping back and forth," Susan says, apparently in his exhilaration for any outdoor experience. But for all the hair-raising ordeals he faced, Enos died in bed at the age of fifty-two, possibly from an infection.

We're nearly at the end as we slip and slide down the mountain. Now is the time to try the downhill techniques we were shown in the beginning. Everyone picks up steam and we sail down the mountain. A few careen through fresh snow, making a trail of their own next to us. By the time we reach the trailhead, the sun is slipping behind the mountains.

The veil of mist has reappeared to halo the mountains and nightfall isn't far away. For those who long for a more extended and difficult climb, the park offers a four-hour intermediate climb, also with a ranger. But now it's time to hunt for hot chocolate, turn in our snowshoes, and leave the snowy park behind.

Rocky Mountain National Park, 1000 Highway 35, Estes Park, 80517; 970-586-1206; www.nps.gov/romo. Entrance fees are $15 for an individual vehicle. On foot or bicycle, motorcycle or horse is $5. Call for reservations at 970-586-1223 between 8 A.M. and 4 P.M. daily. There's a limit of six people for the beginner tour and three for the more challenging tour. Children must be over eight years of age for the beginner program and twelve for the advanced. Children in backpacks are not allowed. Ski poles are recommended for the beginner tour and required for the advanced tour.

Rocky Mountain Nature Association, 1895 Fall River Road, Estes Park, 80517; 970-586-0108 or 800-816-7662; www.rmna.org. Bookstore, field trips, and lectures.

■ **RECOMMENDED READING**

Snowshoeing Colorado by Claire Walter (Fulcrum Publishing, 2000).

■ SOLITUDE IN THE CITY: ROCKY MOUNTAIN ARSENAL NATIONAL WILDLIFE REFUGE

by HEIDI V. ANDERSON

It's a place where bald eagles soar, mule and white-tailed deer cavort, and coyotes compete with foxes for food. Black-tailed prairie dogs squeak at one

Geese on the wing head toward the lakes in their Commerce City haven.

another, while cottontail rabbits rest in their burrows. Grosbeaks, sparrows, orioles, grebes, doves, pelicans, herons, gulls, and dozens of others inhabit the trees and ponds. You could spend an entire day here and rarely see another human being. And this serene, natural retreat is right in the middle of—Commerce City?

Yes, Commerce City, the home of smokestacks and oil refineries, is also the home of one of the most peaceful getaway spots on the Front Range. The Rocky Mountain Arsenal National Wildlife

Refuge is a haven for nature lovers and for those who simply crave a little peace and quiet. And though the refuge is just ten miles from Denver's avenues, it's worlds away in attitude.

AS MUCH HISTORY AS NATURE

A patch of twenty-seven square miles surrounded by civilization, the refuge hasn't always been a sanctuary. It started out that way, of course, before settlers moved west, and even through the 1930s was primarily farmland dotted with houses and barns. But in 1941, with the nation at war, the residents sold their land to the U.S. Government. The Army Chemical Warfare Service tore down most of the existing structures and created South Plants, a facility for manufacturing chemical weapons and incendiary bombs.

As the war wound down, the army leased some of the land to what became the Shell Company, which began production of pesticides and herbicides. And soon after, in the mid-1950s, the government used it as a production facility for the deadly GB nerve agent.

Only a few miles from major cities, the refuge offers space and solitude for people and a sanctuary for wildlife.

The soil, structures, and groundwater were severely contaminated by the time production of the chemicals ceased in 1982. But despite its inauspicious beginnings for wildlife, the center was on its way to becoming a wildlife refuge. In 1986, a biologist discovered a nest of a dozen bald eagles, which at that time were on the endangered species list. The U.S. Fish and Wildlife Service soon entered the picture, discovering that many more species had made the region their home, and the move to protect the area was born.

Today, the Rocky Mountain Arsenal National Wildlife Refuge is filled with prairie grasses and nearly three hundred species, including about two hundred species of birds. Most of the plants are native to the area, although the settlers brought white poplar and other domestic plants to the area. And the birds and mammals have all made their way to the refuge without human aid. The closest the government came to introducing wildlife was when plague killed most of the prairie dogs years ago. The refuge staff relocated prairie dogs from other areas to the refuge, because they are a keystone species on which

Mule deer and white-tailed deer live in close proximity to one another.

nearly every other prairie resident depends, either as a primary food source or by using the towns as shelter or hibernation dens.

A small section of the former arsenal, much like a hole in the middle of a doughnut, is devoted to contamination clean up and is fenced off, but the rest is a national wildlife refuge. Fortunately, the animals were naturally attracted to the buffer zone rather than the industrialized core.

Begin at the Visitors Center

Before you head out into the refuge, your first stop should be the visitors center. Here you can pick up a map of the area that shows the various walking trails, ponds, and other points of interest. If you desire, take a stroll through the kid-friendly Wildlife Learning Lab, where you read about the land's history, watch honeybees at work—if you're lucky, you may see the queen bee—and get as close to a slithery reptile as you'd like. (Their tanks are in a far corner of the room, so you can easily avoid seeing them if doing so will derail you from the day's mission of tranquility.)

A wooden walking bridge conveniently takes visitors over the marshes.

Then, hop on one of the trolley-trams for a two-hour guided tour, or put on comfortable, sturdy shoes and head out on one of the walking paths. The trails and visitors center are well away from remediation sites, so you won't need to worry about disturbing nature's balance.

Once on the trails, you're likely to be inspired to become quiet. Something about the refuge induces you to pay attention to every detail—the shed antlers lying next to a prairie dog's burrow, the tiny raccoon tracks that crisscross a trail, the *peck, peck, peck* of a hungry woodpecker. It's the ideal spot for birdwatchers, and if you listen carefully you can distinguish the calls of scores of songbirds.

Shed antlers alongside a prairie dog's burrow are visual reminders of the surrounding wildlife.

What and whom you see will depend largely on the time of year you visit. When we visited the refuge in February, the bald eagles were nesting, and we were fortunate enough to watch one dive for food in one of the refuge's lakes. In the warmer months, the site blooms with color from cacti and wildflowers such as the Indian blanket flower. Also, while an average of a hundred people a day head out to the refuge on visiting days, you can spend several hours in the trails and not see another human.

If you do wish to meet other visitors, you may want to take part in one of the many free classes the refuge offers.

RESOURCES

Rocky Mountain Arsenal National Wildlife Refuge, **56th Avenue and Havana Street, Building 121, Commerce City, 80022**; 303-289-0232; http://rockymountainarsenal.fws.gov.

RENDEZVOUS WITH RAPTORS: BIRDS OF PREY GET A SECOND CHANCE

by DIANNE ZUCKERMAN

Silent and speckled, the red-tailed hawk sits in a wooden flight cage at the Rocky Mountain Raptor Program (RMRP), the bird's home for the past three months. The hawk is healthy. But it won't be heading back to the wild anytime soon.

A golden eagle is too injured to be returned to the wild but will visit schools as a "teaching" bird.

"He was found by somebody who apparently wanted to keep him as a pet, and his primary feathers on one of his wings were clipped," says Lisa Steffes, the program's coordinator of public outreach. Primary feathers—outer feathers that fan out for landing—do grow back. "But it takes a very long time, a year or more," Lisa explains. While the bird's present confinement is sad, "There's a lot of hope for him. He probably will get back out."

Getting raptors back on their wings is the goal of RMRP, a center for the rehabilitation of injured birds of prey. Located in Fort Collins behind Colorado State University's (CSU's) renowned Veterinary Teaching Hospital, the center treats 150 to 175 raptors a year, about half of which return to the wild. The patients include hawks, owls, kestrels, and eagles. Most suffer from some sort of impact injury—collisions with cars, getting entangled in a fence. Other roughed-up raptors are victims of poisoning, electrocution, or shootings.

"The raptor program started in 1979 as an informal effort of veterinary students to take care of injured birds," director Judy Scherpelz says. Eventually it became a successful student club and, in 1987, Scherpelz was hired to transform the program into a community organization, one in which the general public could become involved and be trained to take care of the birds.

"We have grown significantly since those early days," Judy notes. "In 1987, we had twenty volunteers, we treated maybe twenty or thirty birds a year, and our operating budget…wasn't," she wryly describes the shoestring operation. Today, RMRP has four staff members and one hundred fifty volunteers. Most are CSU students and community members from the Fort Collins area, although some determined volunteers have journeyed regularly from as far away as Denver and Cheyenne, Wyoming.

RMRP's annual operating budget has grown to about $150,000, with primary financial support coming from sales of T-shirts, greeting cards, and other merchandise. Some funds also come from private donations, speaker fees for school and community presentations, and occasional contributions from the Division of Wildlife. CSU provides in-kind support, such as medical care administered by veterinary students, who benefit by learning to take care of wildlife.

EDUCATION MOST IMPORTANT ROLE

The raptor program has two main goals. "We provide medical care, rehabilitation, to get birds of prey back out into the wild," Judy says. "And our second goal is to provide environmental education for the public, to teach people the importance of not only raptors, but wildlife."

"You can rehabilitate one red-tailed hawk and get it back into the wild and help that one red-tail," Lisa adds. "But that isn't going to help the whole population. It's the education that's going to open people's eyes." The key is in "raising awareness that these birds are part of the habitat that we share and that we need to respect that habitat."

A Swainson's hawk spreads his wings in preparation for flying and his imminent release.

Birds destined to visit schools are groomed by volunteers so that they will not fear humans.

It all starts in a modest building where crowded offices play second fiddle to the birds' accommodations. Among several large, newly completed flight cages is a prey guard, a large space where live mice are set loose to monitor a recovered bird's ability to hunt before its release. A dozen smaller wood-paneled enclosures, each about ten feet by twelve feet, include furnishings specific to each bird's need. A bird unable to fly, for example, would have a wooden ramp connecting its perch and the cage's gravel floor.

RMRP's current population includes eleven birds under rehabilitation. Most avian patients come from the surrounding region, although birds have been sent here from as far away as a raptor center in Alaska, which had channels of communication with RMRP and knew the program could provide the required care.

The birds' medical conditions can range from minor scrapes to a need for cutting-edge surgical techniques. Currently, the newest admission is a young great horned owl that "either fell out of a nest or was blown out," Lisa notes. With the arrival of the owl—being treated for a fractured wing—the program has officially begun its seasonal deluge of the "young and dumb," the technical term for wayward baby birds.

Mealtime finds volunteers, who arrive every morning and afternoon to care for the birds, dishing up fresh or frozen mice, hamsters, rabbits, or quail, all of which can get pricey. Mice, for example, can cost up to a dollar each. And a single baby great horned owl can chow down six or more a day.

The center also houses thirty permanently disabled birds, kept as part of the program's educational outreach group. "We treat every bird as a releasable bird, basically, until we prove that we cannot release it," Judy explains. "The education birds, to a certain extent, are the failures from rehab."

Not all birds make good educational candidates. "Some birds are so terrified of people, they can't get past that fear," she notes. Birds that cannot be rehabilitated or are unfit for the education program—for which available cage space is also a consideration—are set aside for euthanasia.

"We need to remember," Judy emphasizes, "that even though we, as humans, don't want to see these beautiful creatures die, what is the quality of life for a wild animal that cannot fly, that is doomed to a life in a cage?"

Some Birds Never Leave

Some of the birds, though, are able to adjust to captivity sufficiently to serve a dual educational purpose. Like the cage of great horned owls waiting to take the newly admitted baby owl under their collective wings, they can function as valuable role models for inexperienced young admissions.

Educational birds, such as a Swainson's hawk that is blind in one eye and can't see well enough to hunt, also are central to the program's outreach efforts, which include area school presentations.

"The look in a second grader's eyes—you see that light bulb go on, and they're just fascinated," Judy describes a reaction that continues to energize her after a decade as director.

To groom the birds for their public appearances, they have a certain amount of interaction with volunteers, who periodically put the birds on their glove-protected fists and take them outdoors. "Some of the birds really like to go for walks and get sunshine," Lisa says. "It's nice for them to see something other than four walls."

Birds being readied for release, however, have as little human contact as possible, to enhance their ability to survive in the natural world. To further improve the odds, releases are timed to coincide with the presence of each type of flock. Whenever possible, raptors are released in the area where they were found.

"One of the best feelings is watching one of the birds fly away," Judy says with a smile. "Just getting away from you as fast as it can."

HOW TO GET INVOLVED

A few of the nonreturnable birds kept as part of the Rocky Mountain Raptor Program's educational component can be seen at CSU's Environmental Learning Center, located at 2400 County Road 9 in Fort Collins. For more about the center, which is open during regular campus business hours, call 970-491-0398.

At present, RMRP's main facility on campus is not large enough to accommodate visitors. "Our real dream is our own new center that would combine caging and the office and work space we need so desperately," Judy says. "A place where the public can come—education facilities, a gift shop on site."

Volunteers take birds that cannot fly outside so that they enjoy the sun and wind.

"Raptors don't have wallets," she says ruefully, adding that their goal is "to get the message to people that if they really care about the welfare of wildlife, of raptors, if they want to make a difference, we need their support."

"We're really proud of our program and feel we offer a very unique resource to the community," Judy says. "We encourage people to get involved. Even if they don't have time to volunteer, [they may] think a little harder about what it is that's flying overhead."

RESOURCES

■ HELPFUL ORGANIZATIONS

Birds of Prey Foundation, 2290 South104th Street, Broomfield, 80020; 303-460-0674;

  www.birds-of-prey.org.

Raptor Protection Program, Boulder Open Space and Mountain Parks, 66 South Cherryvale

  Road, P.O. Box 791, Boulder, 80306; 303-441-3440;

  www.ci.boulder.co.us/openspace/nature/meet_the_species.htm.

Rocky Mountain Raptor Program, Department of Clinical Sciences, College of Veterinary Medicine,

  Colorado State University, 300 West Drake, Fort Collins, 80523; 970-491-0398; www.fortnet.org/RMRP.

■ RAPTOR AND BIRD VIEWING

Barr Lake State Park, 13401 Piccadilly Road, Brighton, 80603; 303-659-6005;

  www.parks.state.co.us.

Where to Bird in Colorado; www.birding.com/wheretobird/Colorado.asp.

Colorado National Monument, Fruita, 81521; 970-858-3617; www.nps.gov/colm. Website

  contains no information about raptors, but the destination is good raptor territory.

Comanche National Grassland, 27162 U.S. Highway 287, Springfield, 81073; 719-523-6591;

  www.fs.fed.us/r2/psicc/coma.

Mesa Verde National Park, P.O. Box 8, Mesa Verde, 81330; 970-529-4465; www.nps.gov/meve.

Pawnee National Grassland, Administrative Offices, 660 O Street, Greeley, 80631; 970-353-5004;

  www.fs.fed.us/arnf/districts/png.

■ RECOMMENDED READING

Careers with Animals by The Humane Society of the United States, written by Willow Ann Sirch

  (Fulcrum Publishing, 2000).

Raptor! A Kids' Guide to Birds of Prey by Christyna Laubach, Rene Laubach, and Charles W.G.

  Smith (Storey Books, 2003).

Raptors of the Rockies: Biology of the Birds of Prey and Species Accounts of the Raptors of the

  Rockies by Kate Davis (Mountain Press Publishing, 2002).

APPENDIX

■ ORGANIZATIONS

Audubon Colorado, 3107B 28th St., Boulder, 80301; 303-415-0130; www.auduboncolorado.org. A major organization for bird lovers.

Colorado Mountain Club, 710 10th Street, Suite 200, Golden, 80401; 303-279-3080; www.cmc.org/cmc. Long-established club offers books and guided tours.

Colorado Mycological Society, P.O. Box 9621, Denver, 80209-0621; www.cmsweb.org. Provides tours to members, also seminars and educational forums on both culinary and non-edible mushrooms.

Colorado Native Plant Society, P.O. Box 200, Fort Collins, 80522; http://carbon.cudenver.edu/~shill/conps.html. Guided tours by members, educational programs.

Colorado Nature Conservancy, 2424 Spruce Street, Boulder, 80302; 303-444-2950; http://nature.org/states/colorado. Worldwide conservation society purchases land deemed essential for wildlife. Seminars at the Zapata Ranch adjoining the Great Sand Dunes National Monument and Preserve and field trips open to members.

Colorado Trout Unlimited, 1320 Pearl Street, Suite 320, Boulder, 80302; 303-440-2937; www.cotrout.org. Educational programs, fishing trips.

Crested Butte Wildflower Festival, 409 Second Street, P.O. Box 216, Crested Butte, 81224; 970-349-2571; www.crestedbuttewildflowerfestival.com. Classes, forums celebrating wildflower display in mid-July.

Denver Botanic Gardens, 1005 York Street, Denver, 80206; 720-865-3500; www.denverbotanicgardens.org. Guided summer tours on Mount Goliath.

Rocky Mountain Nature Association, 1895 Fall River Road, Estes Park, 80517; 970-586-0108 or 800-816-7662; www.rmna.org. Field seminars spring through autumn.

Many of the following sites are visited for several attractions. For example, rock formations also will be home to falcons; wildflower meadows attract hummingbirds. These astonishing places are listed according to their major draw. Each is a climate and topography unto itself.

■ PLACES FOR WILDLIFE

Chatfield Reservoir, 11500 North Roxborough Park Road, Littleton, 80125; 303-791-7275; http://parks.state.co.us/chatfield/index.asp. A popular recreational spot that still is home to herons, owls.

Clear Creek Ranger District Ranger Station, National Forest Service, 101 Chicago Creek Road, Idaho Springs, 80452; 303-567-3000; www.fs.fed.us/arnf/districts/ccrd. Specifics on the Mount Evans Scenic Byway are found at www.mountevans.com. Big horn sheep, marmots, butterflies, bristlecone pines and cushion plants evolved to an alpine setting.

Rocky Mountain Arsenal National Wildlife Refuge, 56th Avenue and Havana Street, Building 121, Commerce City, 80022; 303-289-0232; http://rockymountainarsenal.fws.gov. Deer, coyotes, songbirds, falcons, waterfowl in a prairie environment.

Rocky Mountain National Park, 1000 Highway 35, Estes Park, 80517; 970-586-1206; www.nps.gov/romo. The grand destination for birds, elk, mountain sheep, butterflies, moths, wildflowers, alpine tundra, moose.

■ ROCK FORMATIONS AND FOSSILS

Black Canyon of the Gunnison State Park, 102 Elk Creek, Gunnison, 81230; 970-641-2337 or 970-641-2337, ext 205; www.nps.gov/blca. Secluded canyon of astonishing depth, remarkable views.

Colorado National Monument, Fruita, 81521-0001; 970-858-3617; www.nps.gov/colm. Majestic canyons, ranger-led hikes into the canyon, stunning drive around the rim.

Dinosaur National Monument, 4545 East Highway 40, Dinosaur, 81610; 970-374-3000 or 435-781-7700; www.nps.gov/dino. Dinosaur skeletons have made this site famous, but it's also a wonderfully secluded area of Colorado.

Eldorado Canyon State Park, 9 Kneale Road, Box B, Eldorado Springs, 80025; 303 494-3943; http://parks.state.co.us. Best known by rock climbing enthusiasts, but the canyon also offers wonderful hiking paths, falcons, birds and butterflies.

Florissant Fossil Beds, 15807 Teller County 1, P.O. Box 185, Florissant, 80816-0185; 719-748-3253; www.nps.gov/flfo. Petrified redwoods and detailed fossils.

Garden of the Gods, 1805 North 30th Street, Colorado Springs, 80904; 719-634-6666; www.gardenofgods.com. Popular drive-through site with picturesque rocks.

Rattlesnake Canyon/Arches, Bureau of Land Management, 2815 H Road, Grand Junction, 81506; 970-244-3000; www.co.blm.gov/gjra/rattlesnakearches.htm. Carved arches eroded by wind and water.

Roxborough State Park, 4751 Roxborough Drive, Littleton, 80125; 303-973-3959; http://parks.state.co.us. Famous for both wildlife and rock formations.

■ PRAIRIE

Castlewood Canyon State Park, 2989 South State Highway 83, Franktown, 80116; 303-688-5242; http://parks.state.co.us. Where the Black Forest meets the prairie. Good destination for quiet, solitary hikes.

Comanche National Grasslands, 27162 Highway 287, Springfield, 81073; 719-523-6591; http://www.fs.fed.us/r2/psicc/coma. Remnants of the original prairie before settlers.

Pawnee National Grassland, Administrative Offices, 660 O Street, Greeley, 80631; 970-353-5004; http://www.fs.fed.us/arnf/districts/png. Peaceful prairie set far away from city life.

■ WETLANDS

Barr Lake State Park, 13401 Piccadilly Road, Brighton, 80603; 303-659-6005; http://www.parks.state.co.us. A birder's paradise.

Alamosa/Monte Vista National Wildlife Refuge, U.S. Fish and Wildlife Service, 9383 El Rancho Lane, Alamosa, 81101; 719-589-4021; http://mountain-prairie.fws.gov/alamosanwr/. Destination for those hoping to catch a glimpse of the sandhill cranes.

Great Sand Dunes National Monument and Preserve, 11500 Highway 150, Mosca, 81146; 719-378-2312; www.nps.gov/grsa. Mountains of dunes that shelter an important water system for the surrounding area.

Arapaho National Wildlife Refuge, 953 County Road 32, Box 457, Walden, 80480; 970-723-8202; http://arapaho.fws.gov. The small town of Gould, Colorado, is considered the state's moose-watching destination.

■ WILDFLOWERS

Crested Butte Chamber of Commerce, 601 Elk Avenue, P.O. Box 1288, Crested Butte, 81224;
970-349-6438; www.crestedbuttechamber.com. In July, the surrounding mountains are
blanketed by wildflowers.

Golden Gate Canyon State Park, 3873 Highway 46, Golden, 80403; 303-582-3707;
http://parks.state.co.us. A popular recreation area, also home to wildflowers; yurts available.

■ CULTURAL

Hovenweep National Monument, McElmo Route, Cortez, 81321; 970-562-4282;
www.nps.gov/hove. Smaller and more private than Mesa Verde, located near the border of
Colorado and Utah.

Mesa Verde National Park, P.O. Box 8, Cortez, 81330; 970-529-4465;
www.nps.gov/meve. Large site of ancient American peoples.

■ FOR MORE INFORMATION

Colorado State Parks, 1313 Sherman Street, No. 618, Denver, 80203; 303-866-3437;
http://parks.state.co.us.

■ RECOMMENDED READING

The Colorado Guide, Fifth Edition, by Bruce Caughey and Dean Winstanley (Fulcrum
Publishing, 2001).